Vernacular Dwellings

A Group of Earth Storeyed Buildings in
Nanjing County, Fujian / preceding page

In the mountain areas of southern Fujian, contrasting forms of earth storeyed buildings often co-exist in the same cluster, some round, some square, etc. The photo shows a group of such buildings in the village of Tianluokeng, Shuyang Township, Nanjing County. The surrounding forests, the valley intersected by small rivers, a road winding its way along a stream and the clustered buildings are an attractive sight. This could be the land of Peach Blossoms described by the ancient writer Tao Yuanming. In the photo, the round house to the fore is the Hechang Building; on the left, the Ruiyun Building; the central square one, the Buyun Building. On its right again stands the round Zhenchang Building, the earliest structure in the background. Round storeyed buildings stood for social equality. They could each house an entire clan, and still today remain a favorite architectural form.

The Excellence of Ancient Chinese Architecture

VERNACULAR DWELLINGS

Earth Dwellings,Cave Dwellings and
Siheyuan Compound

Wang Qijun

China Architecture & Building Press

Map of Vernacular Dwellings

交河 ● 交河城遗址（唐）
Jiaohe ● Site of the ancient city of Jiaohe (Tang period)

新 疆 维 吾 尔 自 治 区

新疆维吾尔自治区民宅：
1. 喀什的平顶楼房
2. 和阗的阿以旺民居
3. 伊宁的西亚风格民居
4. 吐鲁番的半地下式住宅
5. 塔什库尔干塔吉克族的垛木天窗顶民居

Vernacular Dwellings in the XinJiang Uighur Autonomous Region:
1. Flat-roofed storeyed buildings in Kashi
2. A'iwang dwellings in Hetian
3. West Asian style in Yining
4. Seimi-subterranean dwellings in Turpan
5. Skylighted log dwelling of the Kazak nationality in Taxhorgan

甘 内 蒙
肃
省

青 海 省

青海
Qinghai

黄

● 兰州

青海省民宅：
庄巢民居
Vernacular Dwellings in Qinghai Province:
"Zhuangchao"tight-enclosed siheyuan

长

省

西藏自治区民宅：
1. 石垒碉房
2. 土筑碉房
Vernacular Dwellings in the Autonomous Region of Tibet:
1. Stone blockhouses
2. Earth blockhouses

Vernacular Dwellings in Sichuan Province:
1. Semi-pile-supported dwellings
2. Through-jointed frame houses
3. Horizontal rectangular compounds

四川省民宅：
1. 吊脚楼
2. 穿斗式屋
3. 横长方形的院落

十二桥商代建筑遗址（商） ● 成都
Chengdu shang period building site at Shi'erq

西 藏 自 治 区

scale
0   100   200   300 km

● Locations of vernacular dwellings
● Locations of municipalities directly under the Central Government, provincial capitals and the governments of autonomous regions

Chinese vernacular dwellings have existed since ancient times, large-sized buildings for clan members living together existied as early as the pre-Qin era. Dwellings of that time fall into two categories: the northern (Yellow River valley), and the southern (Yangtze River valley). The former is represented by the building sites of the Yangshao culture, mostly the remains of shallow semi-subterranean dwellings; the latter, by those of the Hemudu culture, mainly the ruins of pile-supported dwellings. During the Qin and Han periods, when geomancy came into fashion and the Han emperor Wudi advocated Confucianism, the Yin-Yang and Wu Xing (Five Elements) schools and the then ritual system became the theoretical basis for domestic architecture. The compound pattern of layout gradually evolved, with the living rooms in front and the bedrooms to the rear, the left and the right sections symmetrized, and the main house enlarged in size. S toreyed buildings were quits often constructed in contrast to the traditional domestic architecture of the later dynastic periods when dwellings were commonly lower. In the Sui, Tang and Five Dynasty eras, special attention was paid to the ritual system, resulting in a rigid hierarchy both in domestic architecture and the way residences were furnished. As people were accustomed to sitting on the floor, they built relative low houses with spacious bays and wide eaves. During the Song Dynasty, when culture and science made undreamed-of-advances and the scholars-official played a great part in carrying the art of cultivated living still further, architecture was influenced by an aesthetic line of thought that favored a natural and simple approach. As a result, there was little difference between vernacular dwellings and officials' residences. During the Ming and Qing periods, the dominance of the patriarchal system and prevalence of several generations living under the same roof brought about a trend towards larger-sized residence, leading again to the formation of the basic pattern of modern vernacular dwellings.

China's vastness and the wide variety of its topographic, clinatic and cultural conditions have meant that unique types of building developed independently in different regions, such as fortified storeyed buildings in western Fujian and eastern Guangdong, Mongolian yurts inherent in the Mongolian nationality, and cave dwellings in the Central Plains, As there are too many to list completely, only the famous building types include in the present volume are designated on the map.

江

永宁 ● 纳西族井干式住宅
Well frame dwellings of the Naxi nationality

贵

Shang period building site at Haimenkou
海门口商代建筑遗址（商代）● 剑川
Compounds with three fang and a screen wall, and dwellings with four houses and five patios of the Bai nationality
白族"三坊一照壁"与"四合五井"住宅
Pile-supported dwellings at Dabona
大波那干兰式住宅遗址

大理 ●

● 祥云

石板房
Slabston

镇宁 ●
Slabstone

昆明 ●

云南省民宅：
1. 自族民居
2. 井干式住宅
3. 干兰式住宅
4. 一颗印住宅
5. 景颇族长脊短檐民居

云 南 省

Vernacular Dwellings in Yunna Province:
1. Vernacular dwellings of the Bai
2. Well frame dwellings
3. Pile-supported dwellings
4. Seal-shaped dwellings
5. Longer-ridged, shorter-eaved dwellings of the Jingpo

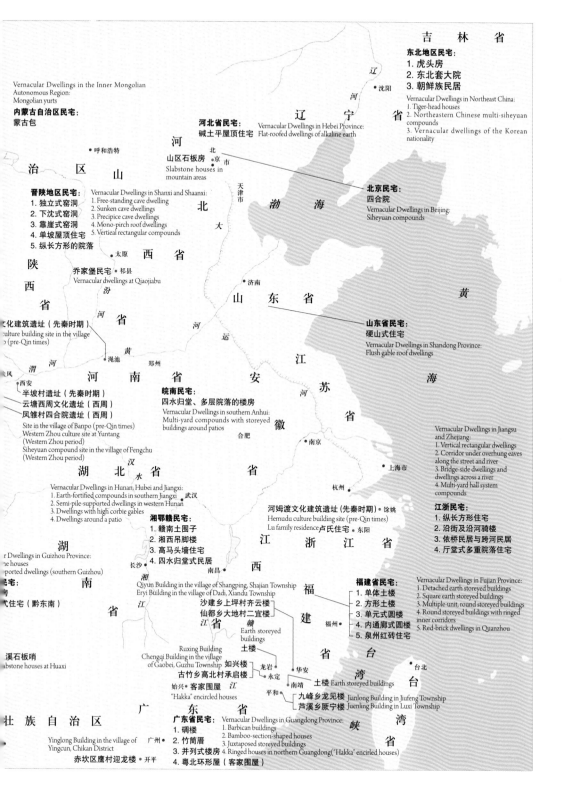

吉 林 省

东北地区民宅：
1. 虎头房
2. 东北套大院
3. 朝鲜族民居

Vernacular Dwellings in Northeast China:
1. Tiger-head houses
2. Northeastern Chinese multi-siheyuan compounds
3. Vernacular dwellings of the Korean nationality

Vernacular Dwellings in the Inner Mongolian Autonomous Region: Mongolian yurts

内蒙古自治区民宅：
蒙古包

辽 宁 省

• 沈阳

辽 河

河北省民宅： Vernacular Dwellings in Hebei Province:
碱土平屋顶住宅 Flat-roofed dwellings of alkaline earth

河

• 呼和浩特

治 区 山

山区石板房 Slabstone houses in mountain areas
北 京 市

北京民宅：
四合院

Vernacular Dwellings in Beijing: Siheyuan compounds

晋陕地区民宅： Vernacular Dwellings in Shanxi and Shaanxi:
1. 独立式窑洞 1. Free-standing cave dwelling
2. 下沈式窑洞 2. Sunken cave dwellings
3. 靠崖式窑洞 3. Precipice cave dwellings
4. 单坡屋顶住宅 4. Mono-pirch roof dwellings
5. 纵长方形的院落 5. Vertial rectangular compounds

陕 西

西 省

天津市

渤 海

大

太原 •

黄

乔家堡民宅 • 祁县
Vernacular dwellings at Qiaojiabu

陕 西 省

• 济南

山 东 省

江

海

文化建筑遗址（先秦时期）
culture building site in the village (pre-Qin times)

黄 河 省 河

汾

黄 河

郑州 •

山东省民宅：
硬山式住宅

Vernacular Dwellings in Shandong Province: Flush gable roof dwellings

西安 •
半坡村遗址（先秦时期）
云塘西周文化遗址（西周）
凤雏村四合院遗址（西周）
Site in the village of Banpo (pre-Qin times)
Western Zhou culture site at Yuntang (Western Zhou period)
Siheyuan compound site in the village of Fengchu (Western Zhou period)

河 南 省 安

皖南民宅：
四水归堂、多层院落的楼房

Vernacular Dwellings in southern Anhui: Multi-yard compounds with storeyed buildings around patios

合肥 •

徽

江

苏

省

河

• 南京

渭 河

湖 北 汉 省

水

武汉

上海市

Vernacular Dwellings in Jiangsu and Zhejiang:
1. Vertical rectangular dwellings
2. Corridor under overhung eaves along the street and river
3. Bridge-side dwellings and dwellings across a river
4. Multi-yard hall system compounds

Vernacular Dwellings in Hunan, Hubei and Jiangxi:
1. Earth-fortified compounds in southern Jiangxi
2. Semi-pile-supported dwellings in western Hunan
3. Dwellings with high corbie gables
4. Dwellings around a patio

河姆渡文化建筑遗址（先秦时期）• 徐姚
Hemudu culture building site (pre-Qin times)
卢氏住宅 • 东阳
Lu family residence

杭州 •

江 浙 民宅：
1. 纵长方形住宅
2. 沿街及沿河骑楼
3. 依桥民居与跨河民居
4. 厅堂式多重院落住宅

湖

r Dwellings in Guizhou Province:
ne houses
ported dwellings (southern Guizhou)

南

宅：
式住宅（黔东南）

湘鄂赣民宅：
1. 赣南土围子
2. 湘西吊脚楼
3. 高马头墙住宅
4. 四水归堂式民居

江 浙 江 省

江 西

南昌 •

福建省民宅：
1. 单体土楼
2. 方形土楼
3. 单元式圆楼
4. 内通廊式圆楼
5. 泉州红砖住宅

Vernacular Dwellings in Fujian Province:
1. Detached earth storeyed buildings
2. Square earth storeyed buildings
3. Multiple-unit, round storeyed buildings
4. Round storeyed buildings with ringed inner corridors
5. Red-brick dwellings in Quanzhou

Qiyun Building in the village of Shangping, Shajian Township
Eryi Building in the village of Dadi, Xiandu Township
沙建乡上坪村齐云楼
仙都乡大地村二宜楼
Earth storeyed buildings

福 建

长沙 •

湘

赣

福州 •

溪石板哨
labstone houses at Huaxi

Ruxing Building
Chengqi Building in the village of Gaobei, Guzhu Township
如兴楼
古竹乡高北村承启楼
"Hakka" encircled houses

土楼

龙岩 •
永定 •

华安 •

南靖 •

平和 •

土楼 Earth storeyed buildings

台北 •

台

湾

台

省

始兴 • 客家围屋

九峰乡龙见楼
芦溪乡厥宁楼

Jianlong Building in Jiufeng Township
Juenling Building in Luxi Township

广

壮 族 自 治 区

东

省

峡

湾

Yinglong Building in the village of Yingcun, Chikan District
广州 •
赤坎区鹰村迎龙楼 • 开平

广东省民宅：
1. 碉楼
2. 竹筒厝
3. 并列式楼房
4. 粤北环形屋（客家围屋）

Vernacular Dwellings in Guangdong Province:
1. Barbican buildings
2. Bamboo-section-shaped houses
3. Juxtaposed storeyed buildings
4. Ringed houses in northern Guangdong("Hakka" encircled houses)

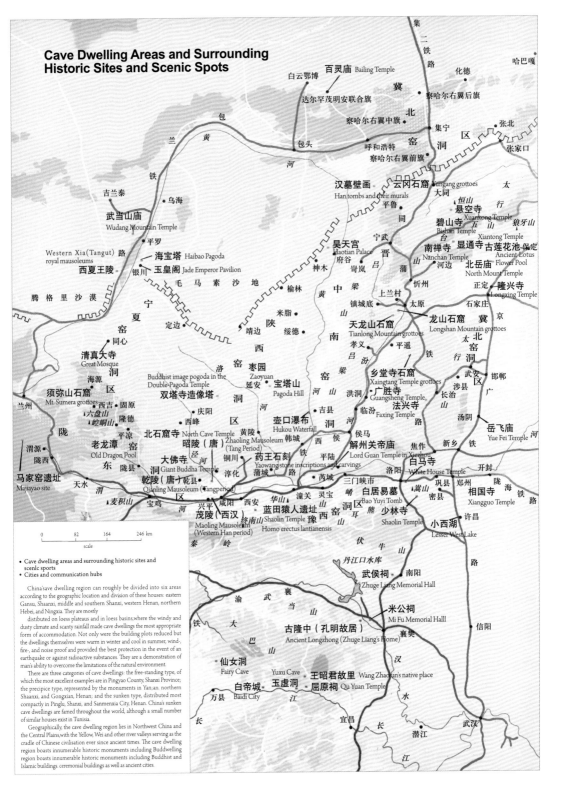

Cave Dwelling Areas and Surrounding Historic Sites and Scenic Spots

scale
0   82   164   246 km

- Cave dwelling areas and surrounding historic sites and scenic sports
- Cities and communication hubs

China's ave dwelling region can roughly be divided into six areas according to the geographic location and division of these houses: eastern Gansu, Shaanxi, middle and southern Shanxi, western Henan, northern Hebei, and Ningxia. They are mostly distributed on loess plateaus and in loess basins, where the windy and dusty climate and scanty rainfall made cave dwellings the most appropriate form of accommodation. Not only were the building plots reduced but the dwellings themselves were warm in winter and cool in summer, wind-, fire-, and noise proof and provided the best protection in the event of an earthquake or against radioactive substances. They are a demonstration of man's ability to overcome the limitations of the natural environment.

There are three categories of cave dwellings: the free-standing type, of which the most excellent examples are in Pingyao County, Shanxi Province; the precipice type, represented by the monuments in Yan;an. northern Shaanxi, and Gongxian, Henan; and the sunken type, distributed most compactly in Pinglu, Shanxi, and Sanmenxia City, Henan. China's sunken cave dwellings are famed throughout the world, although a small number of similar houses exist in Tunisia.

Geographically, the cave dwelling region lies in Northwest China and the Central Plains, with the Yellow, Wei and other river valleys serving as the cradle of Chinese civilisation ever since ancient times. The cave dwelling region boasts innumerable historic monuments including Buddwelling region boasts innumerable historic monuments including Buddhist and Islamic buildings. ceremonial buildings as well as ancient cities.

Contents

General Introduction

Notes on the Photographs

North China

Central China

South China

West China

Appendices

Editor's Note

- The series consists of ten volumes, each of which deals with respectively palace architecture, imperial mausoleums, imperial gardens, private gardens, vernacular dwellings, Buddhist buildings, Taoist buildings, Islamic buildings, ritual and ceremonious buildings and defense structures..

- Each volume is basically composed of four sections, i.e. general introduction, colour photographs, glossary and chronology of major events.

- The general introduction describes the background, development process, architectural characteristics of different types of buildings and is complimented with photographs and drawings.

- The colour photographs are arranged in the order of building distribution area or the time when the building was completed. The series contains about 1,700 exquisite colour photographs, which are attached with captions explaining the location, construction time, and artistic and technical features.

- Each volume is accompanied with layout plan, drawing of recovered buildings, distribution map and travel guide to mark the location of famous buildings and cultural attractions in the vicinity.

- The glossary is arrayed according to the sequence of strokes of Chinese characters, which is a reference for general readers.

- Chronology of major events is affiliated with each volume of the series. Chinese traditional chronology is adopted in the annals of the series, and is also indicated in the Christian era for easy reference.

Preface 1

China enjoys a long and profound history of ancient architecture. Her verifiable artifacts could be dated back to 7,000 years ago from Hemudu ruins in Yuyao to Banpo ruins in Xi'an. Of course, architecture underwent a long process from primitiveness to sophistication before the Warring States, while in the Qin and Han dynasties, it gained an apparent progress along with the development of production and unification of the country. Moreover, in over a thousand years of the prosperous Tang Dynasty to the Ming and Qing dynasties, it reached several unprecedented peaks which were embodied by diversified building forms and refined planning and exquisite construction.

The love of architecture is the love of history and culture. China Architecture & Building Press (CABP), from the very beginning of its founding, has defined the sorting out and publication of traditional Chinese architecture and the enhancement of Chinese culture as one of important themes in its mission. In 1950s and 1960s, many monographs on the subject by experts such as Liang Sicheng, Liu Dunzhen, Tong Jun, Liu Zhiping and others were published. In early 1980s when China was just opened to the outside world, CABP set aside a special fund for publication of academic books on ancient Chinese architecture despite of the limited financial capability then. As a result, large academic albums of Ancient *Chinese Architecture, Ancient Architecture in Chengde, the Art of Chinese Gardens, the Buildings of Confucius Temple in Qufu, Ancient Buildings of Putuoshan, Summer Palace as well as* five volumes of *History of Ancient Chinese Architecture* were put forth continuously. Those books have proved to be of high academic and practical values in consolidation, conservation and protection of the national treasure.

The Excellence of Ancient Chinese Architecture in English is a series of ten volumes on various aspects of the ancient Chinese architecture, which offer a comprehensive coverage of the art, highlighted by the supreme quality of the photos as well as plenty of drawings of plans, sections and perspectives. The easy description would lead to a comprehension of the cultural essence of Chinese architecture, and appreciation of the aesthetics and philosophy embodied by the art. The authors are famous Chinese experts who have long been engaged in the study of the related subjects, whose dedication makes the series authoritative and informative for interested laymen and specialists alike. Now the Excellence of Ancient Chinese Architecture is published. It is a happy event. I believe that it will serve as a door for all those who are interested in the study of ancient Chinese architecture.

Zhou Yi | Former President
China Architecture & Building Press

Former Chairman, Committee on Publication
of Science Books
Vice Chairman, Chinese Association of Publishers

Preface 2

As history advances in the new era of the 21st century, China is once again becoming the focus of worldwide attention. The rich variety of her landscape, the wisdom of her people, the current unprecedented economic growth, and the wealth of her cultural heritage are all becoming the subject of worldwide interest.

In China's extensive and profound cultural treasury, ancient architecture is one of the important components, which, in a sense, is of a symbolic nature. The beauty and elegance of ancient Chinese architecture has a uniqueness of its own in the world architectural system. The strict formality of the city layouts, the lively arrangement of village settlements, the grouping of buildings around courtyards, the comprehensive building code for wood structures, the great variety of colour and architectural form, the perfect harmony of the decorative and structural functions of building elements, the integration of furniture, interior decoration, painting, sculpture and calligraphy into a comprehensive art of architecture, all go to manifest the distinctive characteristics of the traditional Chinese culture. A perusal of the country's magnificent palaces and temples, her tranquil and intricate gardens, the wide variety of her vernacular dwellings, and the exquisiteness of her pavilions and roofed walkways, will lead to a better understanding of China and her people. When one comes to study China's ancient architecture, he will have a deeper comprehension of the oriental philosophy of the "oneness of nature and man" inherent in the architectural forms, as well as of the Chinese people's respect for Confucianism, the expression of their philosophical meditation on time and space through material forms, and their all-embracing aesthetic tastes.

Now the *Excellence of Ancient Chinese Architecture* is published. I believe the vivid and colourful photos will render our readers an enjoyment of aesthetics, and the easy descriptions will facilitate our readers in understanding the cultural essence of ancient Chinese architecture. Under the trend of globalization, it will surely promote the academic exchange internationally and deepen the cultural cooperation among different peoples of the world.

Ye Rutang | Former Vice Minister
Ministry of Construction

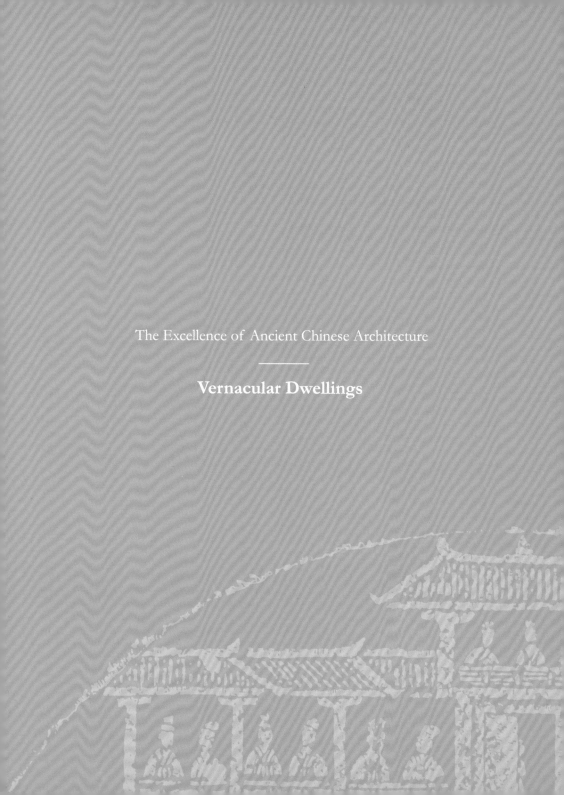

The Excellence of Ancient Chinese Architecture

Vernacular Dwellings

General Introduction

The History of Vernacular Dwellings
—— Their History, Source and Development

History flows by like a deep and silent river. Traditional vernacular dwellings, developed in times technically, economically and culturally far different from today, began to decline when western technical methods such as the use of reinforced concrete started to gain ground. Slowly but surely they are disappearing from the face of this ancient land. Their rich heritage, however, can be drawn upon even today if we concentrate on grasping their inward essence and avoid blindly copying their external appearance. As an ancient Chinese poem exhorts, "Play not music of past dynasties: sing instead the revised song of willow twigs." Only thus can the elegance, grace and artistry of these traditional dwellings be mirrored in those we build today.

I. Vernacular Dwellings of the Pre-Qin Period

The history of vernacular dwellings is very long indeed. In ancient times, when "people were few and beasts were numerous", primitive human beings lived in groups and were so preoccupied with the search for food in order to stay alive that the building of dwellings was of no concern. As stated in the chapter *Xici of Yijing (the Book of Changes)*, "In ancient times, people lived in caves in the wild", and the excavated ruins of caves prove that people in those days did just that, living in caverns in cliffs and forests.

6000-7000 years ago, the matriarchal society in China gradually grew prosperous, and large dwellings emerged occupied by members of a clan. Archaeological excavation has unearthed thousands of ruined dwellings, which may be classified into two categories, the northern and the southern.

The northern category may be represented by the dwellings of the Yangshao culture, first discovered in 1921 in the village of Yangshao, in the county of Mianchi, Henan Province, hence the name. The ruins are distributed over the area of the middle and lower reaches of the Yellow River. Of these, the Banpo village ruin on the east bank of the Chan River is the most famous. According to C14 dating, the Banpo ruin was originated about 4800~4300 B.C., making it

Decorated Bridge at Dipingzhai, Liping County, Guizhou

over 6000 years old. Houses in Banpo style, spread over the area of the middle and lower reaches of the Yellow River, have round or square layouts. Most of them are of the shallow cave type, 50~80 cm in depth and dug into the loess, with steps leading to the interior ground surface. The walls were surfaced with trussed wooden posts, some made very rigid. The ground surface was covered with a layer of straw and clay pressed solid. In the center, a shallow arc-shaped pit served as the fire pit for cooking and heating. The roof was supported by a column at the center. There were also columns around the ground building, which not only supported the roof but also constituted the walling. The roof was covered with straw and clay.

The southern category may be represented by the ruined dwellings of the Hemudu culture first found to the northeast of the Hemudu village of Yuyao in Zhejiang. It is an early Neolithic age culture in the middle and lower reaches of the Yangtze River. Here ruins of Ganlan (pile-supported) type buildings and building parts were discovered. This type building has a wooden or bamboo frame, with the ground floor left empty and people living over it. Ganlan buildings in Hemudu had wooden frames and bark roofs. Joints between beams were of tenon-and-mortise. The dovetails and tenons with holes for pins prevented the wooden frames from slipping out of the joint. The floors were closely matched. These buildings manifested a rather mature technique of wooden frames. Here, a ruin of the earliest wooden structured shallow water well was also found. It was square in shape, each side measuring about 2m, and had a pavilion built

Forms of Dwellings Used by the Primitive Society in Banpo Village, Xi'an, Shanxi

The square dwellings are mostly semi-subterranean, and dug into the loess ground, 50-80 cm in depth and about 20-40 square meters in area. At the entrance is a sloping stepped doorway leading down into the interior and probably with a simple inverted-V-shaped cover on top. Around the shallow pit are walls consisting of wooden posts tied in rows, which support a roof at its edges. In the center of the house, four posts form the skeleton of a roof frame. The roof must have been pyramidal and, in some cases, maybe has a double-pitch top added to provide a source of daylight and let the smoke out. The walls and roof are covered with cob or straw, and the floor surfaced with a layer of compressed cob. The round dwellings are generally built at ground level, 4-6 m in diameter. In the interior are 2,3-6 larger posts; on the periphery, smaller posts are tied in a circle. The roof is conical and presumably has an additional double-pitch top. In the center of the floor is a shallow pit serving as a fireplace for cooking and for warmth. Immediately inside the door, there are two small-sized walls for guiding and restricting airflow so as to control the interior temperature.

Square Dwelling

Cutaway view

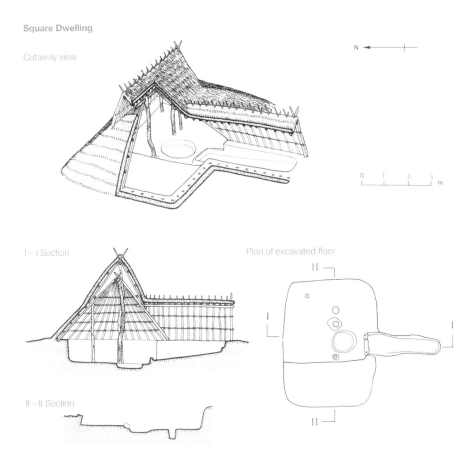

I – I Section

Plan of excavated floor

II – II Section

Cutaway view

Plan of excavated floor

1 Fireplace
2 Carbonized traces of wall posts
3 Partition walls
4 Interior posts

I – I Section

II – II Section

0 1 2 3
             m

N

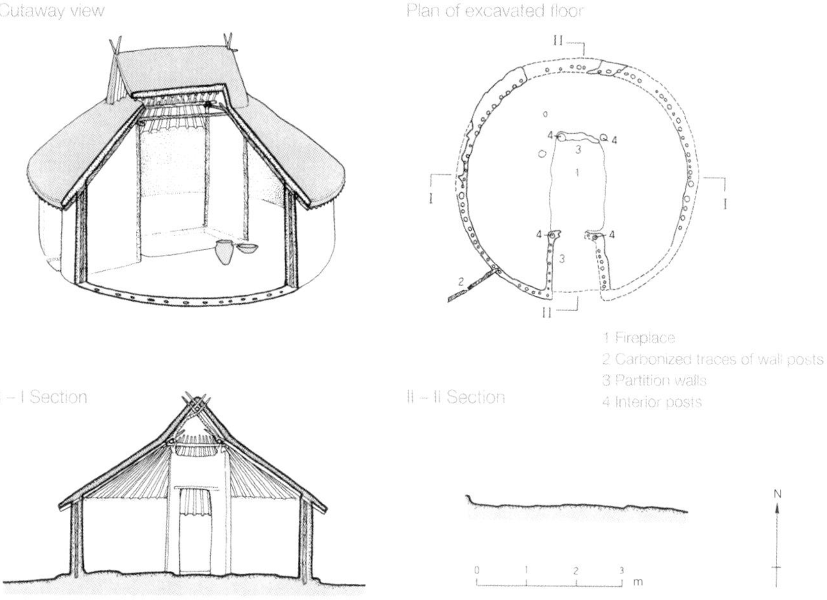

over it. These buildings vary greatly from those of the Yangshao culture of the middle reach of the Yellow River, belonging to another category. According to C14 dating, they were built approx. 4800 B.C., thus making them almost 7000 years old.

When a patriarchal form of society came into being 5000 years ago, housing changed from large buildings for collective dwelling in a matriarchal clan society into small ones for patriarchal family units. As seen from ruins unearthed in some places, there were often several large dwellings intermingled with numerous small ones, indicating that there was already a difference between rich and poor. In addition to semi-underground buildings, buildings above ground were increasing. Improving techniques led to mixed clay and wood constructions being employed, and the method of planning slots and building foundations was mastered. Different types of wall such as that of unfired bricks, banzhu (shutter-rammed) and stone set were also developed. Interior wall surfaces began to be finished with lime-like materials, and attention began to be paid to decoration. Although conditions were extremely hard, ancient man, through his industry,

created a varied culture of building in different parts of the country that has rightly become famous.

During the Shang Dynasty, people had already used numerous bronze tools which greatly facilitated wood construction and the building of clay wall. The latter was called shutter ramming in ancient times. A passage in the second chapter of Gao Zi of the Book of Mencius reads "Fu Yue emerged from banzhu". This was to use wooden planks as side frames, pour loess into the frame cavity and then remove the planks after ramming the loess solid with wooden pestles.

In addition to dwellings above ground, at that time prevalent in the north, there were also some semi-underground vernacular dwellings, while pile-supported type buildings were also widely employed. This is verified by the ruins of buildings of the Shang Dynasty in Shi' erqiao in Chengdu, Sichuan and in Haimenkou of Jianchuan, Yunnan. Characters discovered to have been used during the Shang Dynasty represent the earliest hieroglyphic writing known in China. From some "Jiaguwen" (inscriptions on bones and tortoise shells) related to architecture, we find that buildings were at that time already rich in form. Architectural decorative patterns employed during the Shang Dynasty often had a religious and superstitious flavor. The architecture had a dignified but also mysterious and threatening look, and its religious message is stronger than its aesthetic appeal.

In the Western Zhou Dynasty, the rammed wall of some buildings was overlaid with facing tiles on the exterior and examples of such tiles were

unearthed in Yuntang of Fufeng, Shaanxi. Cleverly designed with nipples at each corner to facilitate attachment to the wall surface, these tiles served to protect the wall from weathering. On the roofs of palaces, ancestral temples and residences of nobles, flat and cylindrical tiles were already in use. The introduction of tiles was a major architectural advancement in ancient China. In the Fengchu village of Qishan, Shaanxi, is a ruin of Siheyuan (a traditional Chinese mansion of the compound type with houses built on all four sides of a courtyard and usually without windows in the enclosing walls), being the earliest known in China. Also discovered at the southeast corner of the building was a sewage system consisting of earthenware pipes or set pebbles. This practice of having a sewage exit at the southeast corner of a dwelling continued until the Ming and the Qing Dynasties. Shutter ramming, the common method of building during the Shang Dynasty, was superseded in the period of Spring and Autumn and that of the Warring States by pile-supported. We know from descriptions in the literature of the Zhou Dynasty as well as in *Zhouli (the Ritual of Zhou), Shijing (the Book of Poems)* and *Shangshu (the Book of Ancient Time)* etc., in addition to excavated testimonies, that not only were the dwellings and palaces of these two periods already on quite a large scale but that they had gate houses, multiple eaves and crisscross latticework over the windows. In the first chapter *Chuyu of the book Guoyu (Record of Speeches in Various States)*, there is a passage reading "High civil works are appropriately rendered beautiful by red paint and carvings", indicating that people at that time were already paying attention to the spiritual implication of buildings. As already mentioned, buildings at that time were mostly of pile-supported type in structure. Floors inside the building were higher than ground level outside, and those entering had first to take off their shoes. The mat seats were located close to the door, and these were used for kneeling on. Beneath them were bamboo room mats, used for measuring the square volume of a room. In *the Kaogongji (the Survey on Construction Work) of Zhouli*, one could read, for instance, "For the king , each room is also of two". Dwellings were further developed in the period of Warring States. Beds were commonly used for sitting-on or lying on to rest. At that time, beds for sleeping were very low but very large, and most peculiarly, were surrounded by balustrades. The building itself was painted, and the color used reflected the owner's position in the social hierarchy. The titles on the eaves were decorated with beautiful reliefs of Taotie (a kind of legendary beast), whirls of water and curled clouds.

In the southern part of China at that time, storeyed pile-supported type houses prevailed. Basement space was much more extensive than that provided in platform pile-supported type houses in the North. Two small and elegant bronze models of pile-supported type houses dating from the period of the Warring States and unearthed in the village of Dabona, Xiangyun, Yunnan, are highly expressive. They show the lower floors to be spacious while the upper ones projecting, have window openings and xuanshanding (overhang gable-end roofs). Their decorative interweaving and twisting has something in common with the literary style of the time, showing how different art forms can influence each other given the same social and aesthetic background. The Survey on Construction Work of Zhouli maintained that "Time belongs to heaven, air belongs to earth, skill belongs to workmanship and quality belongs to the materials. Only through a combination of the four can high quality be obtained." Reference was made to the extremely important concept of the correlation of the four factors of time, space, technique and materials.

The achievements of the pre-Qin architecture were notable, exemplified in particular by the quality of the modeling of wooden frames and the capacity to appeal to the imagination. It was an architecture that was oriental in style very different from that of ancient Greece and mirrored the aesthetic conscience and ideals of the period.

II. Vernacular Dwellings of the Qin, Han and Two Jin Dynasties

Although short, the Qin Dynasty played a vital role in the development of China. The six states were unified, creating a large, centralized empire, decentralized states were organized into unified prefecture and county), and the characters as well as the system of weights and measures were unified. As far as architecture was concerned, the move of 120,000 rich and powerful families of the six states to the capital city of Xianyang was a boost to culture in general and architecture in particular.

During Qin and Han, Fengshui (a form of geomancy) began to develop. According to this system, Yijing and bagua (the eight diagrams) are taken as a means of Fengshui, which is based on the theory of qi (energy), that of yin (negative) and yang (positive) and that of wuxing (five elements), and was used to discover the ideal location for a building. Fengshui was based on a very ancient wisdom. In addition, in the reign of Wudi Emperor of the Han, Confucianism was held in high esteem and all the other 5 disciplines were rejected. As a result, integral order, a ritual system of facades and configuration became key elements of vernacular dwellings. Buildings became more rigid in style, less flexible and showed less variety. The Han Dynasty dwellings, for instance, consisted of a high and large main house with the main room in front and the bedroom to the rear, symmetrical left and right sides and a courtyard, and interestingly have undergone very little change since. The literary records indicate what form Han Dynasty buildings took, but it was the large number of unearthed cultural relics, such as pictures on stones and bricks, funerary earthenware houses, bronze houses, etc. that have provided figurative information and fascinating details.

The unit of dwellings most commonly used in the Han Dynasty, especially the Western Han Dynasty, is the system of one large room and two inner chambers which was also the system preferred by the common people. The size of inner chamber was generally a square zhang (approximately $11m^2$). The size of the large room is twice that of inner chamber, so the layout of the house is nearly a square, like the character田, such a house system of double bays is commonly found in funerary articles, ancestral temples and rock tombs.

The layout of smaller-scale dwellings was square or rectangular, with the door of the house either at the center of one of the sides of the house or deviated to one side. Wooden frames were mostly employed for the structure, a solid wall structure being rarely used, and the walls consisted of rammed earth.

Illustration of the Forms of Dwellings During the Han Period

Pile-supported dwelling
Funerary model of a house from a Han tomb in
Guangzhou, Guangdong

Dwelling 日 - shape in plan
Funerary model of a house from a Han tomb in
Guangzhou, Guangdong

Sanheyuan-style dwelling
Funerary model of a house from a Han tomb in
Guangzhou, Guangdong

L – shaped dwelling
Funerary model of a house from a Han tomb in
Guangzhou, Guangdong

Superficies of Residences

Storied building and verandas
Pictorial stone from Shuanggou, Suining, Jiangsu

Gate
Pictorial brick from Deyang, Sichuan

Dwelling
Pictorial stone from Shuanggou, Suining, Jiangsu

Compound
Pictorial brick from Deyang, Sichuan

Windows could be square, horizontally rectangular or circular. Roofs were of the overhang gable-end or shallow vault-type. Single-or multi-storeyed dwellings on a slightly larger scale were provided with walled courtyards. In the Han Dynasty, the practice of living in storied buildings was common, in contrast to later times. (Nowadays, there are still storeyed buildings in the southwest and southeast, but in northern China most buildings are single-storeyed.) The vogue of living in storeyed buildings was obviously to slightly raise the lower section of the pile-supported type buildings so that it could be used as the main room while people still lived upstairs. But, owing to the fact that in the north the climate was cold and windy, wooden storeyed buildings were not suitable and later gradually decreased in number. Pile-supported type buildings still prevailed during the Han Dynasty. The saying "sitting on the mat on the ground" has its origins in the custom of doing just this in pile-supported type dwellings. Further evidence that this type of house prevailed during the Han Dynasty has recently been found in funerary articles excavated in Guangzhou.

There were, during this period, buildings of a multi-storeyed kind that nearly every well-to-do family or big landlord had. These were the wanglou, or jiaolou, used as a watchtowers. In case of alarm, people could climb up it and beat the drum to call for help. Earthenware watchtowers were often found in Han Dynasty tombs. There were various forms of three, four and five storeys. Most of them are double-or single-bay. Each floor had eaves above and balustrades of sitting height below. Some of the walls were wholly color-painted. It is interesting to note that the structure of wooden pagodas was developed from these. Watchtowers may be used as a reference for today's design of high-rise buildings. All dwellings of better quality built during the Han Dynasty had flights of steps to the left and right. The left one was used by the host for ascending and descending, while the right one was used by guests, as was the custom during the period of Spring and Autumn and that of the Warring States. One was expected to take off one's shoes when entering the house, and then sit on the floor.

During this period, beds extended in function and came to be used for everyday activities and for receiving guests. They were accompanied by low tables and had screens behind them and on each side. For the elderly and those held in high esteem a kind of narrow and low bed called ta (couch) was still in use, and generally had canopy. The four walls were hung with curtains. The chapter *Chen She Shijia (Biography of Chen She)* in *Shiji (the Book of History)* tells

Ceramic Funerary House of the Han Dynasty

The architectural forms of dwellings in the Han Dynasty cannot be verified by records in literature only, but also can be understood in more detail through figurative materials provided by unearthed cultural relics as pictorial stones and bricks, ceramic funerary houses, bronze funerary houses etc. Structures of houses in the Han Dynasty, except a few with bearing wall structures, most adopted wooden frame structure. Walls were built with rammed earth. Forms of windows were various as square, rectangular, circular, etc.

Funerary Sheep Pen with Green Glaze in the Han Dynasty

The pen is rectangular in shape with walls and houses all around. There are 15 big and small sheep and two shepherds in the pen. A dog is guarding outside the door. All are vivid in attitude. From this we can see the condition of farming activities in the Han Dynasty.

us of "seeing the hall and curtains on entering the room". Interior decoration of this nature was by then very common. A passage from *Gaodiji (Biography of Gaoti)* in *Han Shu (the History of the Han Dynasty)* reads, "planning and deploying within the bed, while determining victory in the battle a thousand Li away". There were five basic types of roof used during the Han Dynasty, namely: the xuanshan roof (overhang gable-end roof), the wudian roof (hipped roof), the tunding roof (shallow-vaulted roof), the xieshan roof (gable-and-hipped roof) and the zuanjian roof (pavilion roof). A multiple-eaved roof, too, emerged through combining the hipped roof and piyan (projecting eaves). In ancient Chinese architecture, roofs were most typically grand in scale. A roofscape of a mixture of styles gently interwoven and expressing both magnificence and grace, simplicity and lightness, was a wonderful sight, and had a subjective appeal to the imagination. Although styles developed somewhat in later ages, the basic forms remained the same. Thus, dwellings in the Han Dynasty expressed a certain naivety and ingenuousness, but they were neither dull nor crude in style. Spatially, they were compact but also showed variety and richness of structure. Artistically, many a new style was created and it can be said that a relatively high standard was reached.

The period of Wei and Jin saw new ideas emerge, which were upheld by the scholar-official and the literati: sensitivity towards nature, a romantic attitude and a certain open-mindedness. The architecture of the period also reflected such ideas. Many houses at that time had windows in rows with straight latticework and bamboo or textile curtains, so that the world outside was partly visible. Corridors ran inside the walls around the courtyard, and inverted-V corbel brackets, left natural, and simple in form, were mounted under the eaves. The employment of such brackets continued from the end of the Han Dynasty to that of the Tang. The entrance doorway of some aristocratic houses had hipped roofs with ridge-ends of celestial animal head, however, were only allowed for palaces and not for dwellings unless permission had been granted. Inside, a platform was constructed using short columns and square lumbers to form a wooden frame over which planks were laid. On top of these, mats for sitting on were spread. Customary at the time, as one can see in the Nushizhentu (Portrait of a lady) by Gu Kaizhi of East Jin, was to sit cross-legged. The era of the Northern and Southern Dynasties was an important transit period continuing the two Han dynasties and succeeded by Sui and Tang. During this period, continual wars and frequently changing dynasties resulted in life being hard and turbulent for each and everyone. Buddhism naturally became the spiritual sustenance of the people. There was a tendency for the intellectual to escape from worldly affairs and the society, and as a result the architecture of vernacular dwellings had a tranquil, detached, even mysterious air.

III. Vernacular Dwellings of the Tang and Song Periods

Tang, Song and the Five Dynasties were a period when new and fascinating developments were made. The art of vernacular dwellings rose to an unprecedented height.

Even prior to the period of Warring States, Books such as Zhouli and Yili had already stipulated in written form the system of rites, but it was not until the Sui, Tang and the Five Dynasties that residences were controlled by sumptuary law. Entrance doors, for instance, of aristocrats took the form of Wutou (black

Vernacular Dwellings in Shexian County, Anhui

Quite many examples of vernacular dwellings of the Ming Dynasty remain up to now, some of really large scale. Owing to development of brick-making industry, proportion of vernacular dwellings with brick structure was greatly increased. Though many vernacular dwellings were yet of timber structure, timber pillars were enclosed by brick-laid wall, changing the external appearance of vernacular dwellings.

head). As recorded in the chapter *Yufuzhi (Systems of Living Facilities)* of *Tanghuiyao (Systems in the Tang Dynasty)*, "For officials of more than the fifth rank, the main house should not exceed five bays and seven frames, and the hall should be at both ends. The door house should not exceed three frames. A black head entrance door should generally be constructed." Ordinary buildings, such as the storeyed pavilion-type building of the Han Dynasty, were on the decline.

Youchuntu (Picture of Touring in Spring) by Zhan Ziqian of the Sui Dynasty depicted country dwellings with the siheyuan of narrow rectangular layout surrounded by houses in a beautiful and quiet setting, the whole enhanced by the gently undulating roofs. The sanheyuan, a fenced compound consisting of thatched houses built on three sides of a yard, the fourth being taken up by a wall, is compact in layout. The wall here is of carved wood, and allowed the sighing of the wind in the forest of pine trees even to be heard in the hall. The compound, with its lingering charm and carefree and content air, displays a similar lightness and elegance to Lushan Caotang (Lushan Thatched Cottage) of Bai Juyi, the famous Tang Dynasty poet.

In *Jiutangshu (the Old Book of the Tang)*, there are many detailed descriptions of the dwellings of aristocrats. Tang Dynasty frescoes discovered in a cave in Mogao provide excellent illustration of such dwellings, with corridors zigzagging their way through the courtyard, and fine tiles covering the undulating roofs of the buildings surrounding it. The poem *Shangzhai (Lament of a Building)* by Bai Juyi reads, "Who erected this building / With red door by the avenue / Grand houses arranged like teeth of a comb / High walls meandering / There are altogether seven halls / Beams and eaves being adjacent to each other", giving the reader a wonderful insight into the elaborate of such dwellings.

Worth mentioning is the fact that although the custom of sitting on the floor and using beds or couches was still widely practised from the Sui, Tang to the period of the Five Dynasties , the custom of sitting with one's legs pointing downwards began to be popular among the aristocracy, spreading to the whole country. It was towards the end of Tang and during the period of the Five Dynasties that the types of furniture that continued to be used in later periods too began to bedeveloped. The disposal of indoor space and the design of rooms too, began to change. By the time of the Five Dynasties, dwellings of some aristocratic residences were already very different from popular dwellings, with floors for sitting on and sliding doors.

Nothing remains of the magnificence and prosperity of the old Tang cities, but a remarkable record of the planning of the city of Chang'an in the form of a stone map and accompanying text dating from 1081 has come down to us. The fang-li system was adopted for the city, and although planning followed the system used during the Han Dynasty, and that used in Luoyang of the Northern Wei Dynasty, it was now on a much larger scale. Inside the high walls and gates of the fang residential areas, people were safe from attack and robbery. The main streets ran outside the fang. In the case of large fangs, doors were provided on all four sides, while in smaller ones, doors were set only in the eastern and western walls. In the Jiaohe City, Xinjiang, the approximate shape of the old city as it was during the Tang Dynasty can still be seen today due to the dry climate and its rare rainfall. Large, high walls of earth were erected on both sides of the street, and gates into the fang were only to be found in small alleys. Only going through the gate did one come to the door into the court. This fang-li system had the same configuration as that of Central China. Records tell us that the fangs were closed at night and patrolled by guards.

The fang-li system was not abolished until the Northern Song in Bianjing when the night time bazaars characteristic of economically more prosperous times could not be forbidden. Each residence in the fang-li was in turn encircled with high walls. A residence at that time was therefore surrounded and protected by at least three types of wall, namely: the city wall, the fang wall and the courtyard wall. Within the courtyard, one could reach the bedroom only by going through a series of doors such as the entrance door an intermediate door and the hall door. The fang-li system not only provided security but also intimacy, and the use of walled courts with their natural-looking gardens lent a magnificent and solemn air to the city as a whole. Thus, the architecture of the Tang Dynasty was already highly developed. This period took the vernacular dwelling much further as far as art, technique and scale were concerned.

In the Northern Song, the fang-li system was abolished, but residences were

Patio of a Residence in Shexian County, Anhui

Patios in vernacular dwellings in southern Anhui are generally not very big. The floor is paved with stone slabs to facilitate cleaning. Vernacular dwellings in southern Anhui are cool and elegant, presenting an air of extreme cleanness and leisure.

still controlled by sumptuary law. *Yufuzhi of Songshi (History of Song)* stipulates that "The residences of princes in office are called Fu, those of other officials Zhai and those of common people Jia." Ample evidence of Song residences has come down to us in illustrative form. Compared with the strength and grandeur of Tang vernacular dwellings, those of the Song Dynasty were less magnificent, but possessed a simple and natural beauty all of their own. The sentiments expressed in "the sense of quietness and indifference towards fame and wealth" and "the mind of mildness and calmness" are reflected in the architecture of the period.

Qingmingshanghetu, a painting by Zhang Zeduan of the Song Dynasty depicts urban life in the Northern Song capital of Dongjing, also called Bianliang. In the picture, farmers house outside the city are relatively crude and simple: some are huts with low wall, some are thatched or tile-covered houses. For urban dwellings, overhung gable-end or gable-and hipped roofs were employed. Bamboo booths are shown constructed in front of the projecting eaves, adding a further dimension to the roofs. House corner structures are particularly fine. The main ridges of two sides of the house are often prolonged to form two transom windows crossing perpendicularly. The mutually hooked form is often applied to the door houses of the siheyuan so that the roof curve produces a splendid effect. Trees and flowers are planted in the garden, a carefree and leisurely atmosphere.

In the rural scene depicted in the painting of "Vast Land" by Wang Ximeng of the Northern Song Dynasty, there are many dwellings, most of which possess courtyards with wall consisting mainly of bamboo fences and wooden pilings. Entrance doors of various forms are shown. There are rooms to the left and right. Most of the vernacular dwellings are generally "工" shaped houses consisting of the front hall, the through corridor and the rear bedroom. All in all, these dwellings convey a leisurely atmosphere, making one want to linger. Outside the residences of aristocrats and officials, wutoumen (black-head gates) or door house was constructed, and in the case of the later, the "interrupted laying" method was often employed in the middle bay to allow for the passing of carts and horses. Gallery house often took the place of the winding corridors in order to increase living space, the siheyuan thus changed in function and appearance. The layout of the dwellings with its underlying principle of "main room in front and bedroom to the rear" introduced during the Han Dynasty remained unchanged, except for the fact that now through galleries were

The Rural Dwellings Painted in the "Vast Land" by Wang Ximeng of the Song Period

Small-Sized Dwelling

Medium-Sized Dwelling

Large-Sized Dwelling

Village

constructed to connect the hall for reception and sitting room and the bedroom to the rear, resulting in a "T" shaped, "工" shaped or "王" shaped plan, with lateral rooms or courts on either side of the hall and bedroom. Houses were mostly overhung gable-end in form, and decorated with both ridge and wall beasts. In spite of the fact that in Northern Song period the use of dougong (corbel bracket), caissons, door houses and painted wooden beams were only allowed for officials' residences and palace temples in an effort to maintain the feudal system of hierarchy, the law was on occasion ignored by landlords and rich merchants.

In the period of the two Song dynasties, the custom of sitting with legs pointing downward at last replaced that of kneeling, practised since Shang and Zhou times. Furniture in daily use at, or on which one sat, such as tables and chairs now became highly popular. This new type of furniture also led to pile-supported floors in vernacular dwellings being superseded by ones of earth as well as to a change in the shape of houses. High and slender forms replaced the former lower heights and deeper depths, and the height of the latticework windows also increased. It is only in Korea that dwellings designed

Zhu's Residence in Village of Xucun, Huoxian County, Shanxi

Traditional Chinese domestic architecture was restricted in many aspects. For example, lacquer, color painting and corbel bracket supporting were prohibited in the construction of vernacular dwellings. Nevertheless, some residences were exquisitely decorated. Zhu's Residence in the photo is strictly configured. The semicircular arches above and rectangular windows below implies that "the heaven is round and the earth square." Carved wooden patterns on the decorated brackets are complex in color and inlaid with gold and full of carvings and paintings; brick engravings on the eaves of the architrave are rich in images and strongly stereoscopic.

for the custom of sitting on the floor, dating from the Tang Dynasty are still to be seen.

Important changes also took place in the structure and modelling of furniture. The box-shaped structure prevailing in the Sui and Tang eras was replaced by post-and-beam framing, and decorative moldings were now extensively used, together laying the foundation for further changes in the Ming and Qing periods.

This was the time when the aesthetic ideology of the literati and scholar-officials, its main characteristic of the pursuit of unaffected and natural beauty, increasingly began to influence taste in general. This aestheticism differed greatly from that of the governing class which was primarily interested in the bombastic and the excessively decorated. At this point, the difference between these two groups was especially obvious and influenced later generations. Thereafter, the contrast between vernacular and official buildings became even more marked, and their styles differed increasingly. Vernacular dwellings of the Song Dynasty thus possessed a refined and clear artistic style.

IV. Vernacular Dwellings of the Ming and Qing Periods

The scale of vernacular dwellings of the Ming Dynasty exceeded that of their predecessors by far. Owing to the prevalence of the patriarchal clan system, large families were very common. There were indeed many families which had members of three or four generations living together and sharing the property. Family conflicts were dealt with in the clan hall. Some vernacular dwellings of the Ming Dynasty still exist, some on a very large scale indeed. The development of brick-making meant that brick-built buildings greatly increased, and although there were still many with a wooden structure, the fact that wooden pillar were encased by brick wall led to the outward appearance of dwellings changing; beautiful nonetheless, in a different way from the earlier wooden buildings. The strict hierarchical system for dwellings continued in the Ming Dynasty, but as mentioned above, many powerful officials, rich merchants and landlords defied the law and had residences built on a grand scale, descriptions of which can be found in literature. These would, for instance, possess over one thousand rooms and have beautiful gardens extending over several li. One of the largest extant house complexes is that which belonged to the Dongyang Lu family, who were high officials serving the Ming court. The mansion, with its elaborate arrangement of commemorative gateways (pailous) grew over several generations to become a residence of breathtaking size and luxury. It was also during the Ming period that the earliest storeyed house of the unit type emerged. Qiyunlou in the village of Shangping, Shajian Township in the county of Hua'an, Fujian Province, a storeyed building oval in shape was built in the 18th year of the reign of Wanli (1590 AD) of the Ming Dynasty, and the round building with outer walling of bond granite, Shengpinglou, was built in the 29th year of the reign of Wanli (1601 AD). These two buildings are both earth storeyed buildings of large dimension with a courtyard at the center and the ring-formed building on the perimeter divided into one or two dozen units. Each living unit has its own kitchen, small courtyard, hall, bedroom and sitting room, forming separate living spaces. According to the family tree of the clan, the history of Qiyunlou may be traced back to the fourth year of the reign of Hongwu in the Ming Dynasty (1371 AD). In other words, in China, unit type storeyed buildings emerged as early as over 600 years ago.

Many types of Ming Dynasty dwellings are extant. These are: the yaodong (cave dwelling), the siheyuan in the northern regions, the closed court in the

southern regions, the earth storeyed buildings in Fujian, the southern pile-supported storeyed dwelling and the yikeyin-type dwelling in Yunnan, etc. The main features of the vernacular dwellings of the Ming Dynasty, during which great advancements were made, were an emphasis on naturalness and on providing a framework conducive to greater personal spiritual freedom. Local versions of the basic forms appeared in various places. Within the scope permitted by the system at that time, vernacular dwellings allowed aesthetic interests and individual requirements for freer development, more or less breaking with the ethical and moral limitations of the time.

The technique of ramming earth, colored glaze, carpentry, the brick arch were all greatly developed in the Qing Dynasty, but vernacular dwellings changed little as far as the architecture was concerned. In the period from the middle-Ming to the Opium War, democracy was in its embryonic stage. Although it was at first limited to a few places in the southeast, it was to have far-reaching consequences, in particular those of an ideological nature, for the

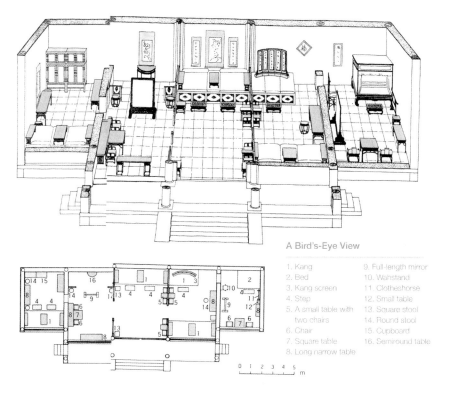

A Bird's-Eye View

1. Kang	9. Full-length mirror
2. Bed	10. Washstand
3. Kang screen	11. Clotheshorse
4. Step	12. Small table
5. A small table with	13. Square stool
two chairs	14. Round stool
6. Chair	15. Cupboard
7. Square table	16. Semiround table
8. Long narrow table	

whole of Chinese society. Social life was also to undergo significant change. A history of vernacular dwellings shows that each era brought about change, sometimes decisive, sometimes less so. The Song, Jin and Yuan dynasties saw much experimentation in wooden frames and modeling. Yueliang (a crescent-shaped beam, a slightly arched beam in the beam of a round-ridged roof), duanqifa (the technology of interrupted brick-laying), the asymmetrical joint of roof trusses, 工 and 王 shaped layouts, etc. with through galleries had all contributed towards taking the art of building further. However, it was during the Ming and Qing dynasties that the large wooden structure of vernacular dwellings was simplified and gradually fell into a pattern. The gently flowing lines of many of the roofs in Central China disappeared, to be replaced by a relatively serious and simple style. Fashionable in the Kangxi and Yongzheng period especially was the ornamentation inside vernacular dwellings. The efang (architrave) and the zhuchu (column plinth) were all richly carved. Delicately carved and intricately patterned were the shanhua (pediment) on the shanqiang

(gables) of the yingshanding (flush gable roof, two-sloped roof flush with the gables or slightly lower). It was then as well that ground brick walls were often installed at both ends of the corridor running under the eaves. In vernacular dwellings in the south, emphasis was even laid on giving the fire-sealing gables visual variety, adding a certain brilliance to the whole. The chuihuamen (a pendant floral gate, the second gate of an old-style mansion with a vaulted top and carved, painted ornamentation) of the siheyuan in the north were heavily painted and possessed subtle elegance. In addition to the interior embellishment of vernacular dwellings, furniture in the Qing Dynasty was perfectly crafted and possessed an artistic quality that in the strength and homogeneity of its style was highly impressive.

The artistic features of vernacular dwellings in the Qing Dynasty were vigorous in form and of fine craftsmanship. Doors and windows and the efang, zhuchu and shanhua were all heavily ornamented. Inspired by the prevailing taste for the heavily decorated, it sometimes inevitably lead to a certain emptiness and meaninglessness, and the standard of architecture exceeded that of previous periods by far. There are many examples of Qing Dynasty architecture still extant, some of them in good condition.

The furniture of both the Ming and Qing dynasties was displayed above

all a good choice of material, not only giving full play to the actual properties
of the material, but also allowing its color and texture to be utilized at best
and thus achieving unity of form and texture. The method used in the frame
type structure conformed with the principles of mechanics, and at the same
time, gave the piece a graceful, three-dimensional profile. It was often only
the subsidiary parts that were carved, resulting in a decorative effect without
weakening the stability. Altogether, the furniture impressed by its stability,
harmonious proportions, clear lines, its dignity and at the same time its liveliness.
From the pre-Qin period to the beginning of the last century, it was the wooden
frame structure that provided the structural basis for the main body of the
building. Although through the ages different styles had appeared in different
versions depending on the part of the country, in the main there had been no
radical break-through as regards the architecture. In this, Chinese vernacular
dwellings differed from those of the west, and played an important part in
Chinese traditional culture and its philosophy. The richness and multiformity of
Chinese vernacular dwellings is a crystalization of the times, which is extremely
precious, and the values derived from studying and understanding this priceless
heritage cannot be overestimated.

Building Forms of Vernacular Dwellings
—— Residences Implying Public Awareness, the Style
Conforming with Local Conditions

Developed over generation, Chinese traditional vernacular dwellings came to have a standard form: the principal component being a wooden frame house surrounded by a court. Styles of buildings varied, some of which are unique in the world, and the forms of layout were also multifarious.

I. Classification of Layouts

To create order in space has to do with the artistic aspects of architecture, while the composition involved is determined by the layout of the buildings. The layout of vernacular dwellings in China manifests a high aesthetic sense of space, the variation of planes rich in connotation and displaying a mental adroitness on the part of the builder. The inherent beauty of the layout has many aspects: a masculine vigor, a dreamy ambiguousness, romantic independence and an innocence associated with a feeling for naturalness. The arousal of such different emotions in the onlooker is all the more surprising when one considers that the layout of vernacular dwellings has a simple and almost naive language all of its own, resulting from the dexterous combination of such simple forms as squares, circles, rectangles and rings. The way in which the language of architecture was used in the layout of vernacular dwellings to appeal to such a variety of emotions is surely unique.

1. The Lateral Rectangular Plan

The lateral rectangular plan is the basic form for small scale dwellings in China, courtyard dwelling being composed of individual lateral rectangular dwellings.

This type of layout was the most commonly used for vernacular dwellings. A building could have one to six or seven rooms depending on the scale of lateral extension. The form of layout followed the same pattern with the longer side facing south, and doors and windows installed in the south-facing wall in order to gain maximum sunshine and minimize as far as possible the effects of cold northern winds. In the case of small dwellings with a width of one or two bays, the location of doors and windows was more or less left free, but in larger houses with a width of three bays and over, the open bay was generally positioned in the center, and a symmetrical form adopted for the left and right sides. Taking a house with seven bays for example, the names of bays from the center to the left and right are: the central bay (the section between the two central columns in the facade of the building) or tangwu (also called zhengfang, the main building on the principal axis of a mansion), the sub-central bay (one of the two sections between the central bay and the end ones of a building), shaojian (the bay between the sub-central bay and the end bay) and jinjian (one of the end rooms of a seven-bay building).

2. The Longitudinal Rectangular Plan

Longitudinal rectangular plans were popular for small-scale dwellings. Such forms of layout were narrow in width but generous in depth, Temporary small houses for supervising crops in the north and some

Vernacular Dwellings in Qianjiazhai, Xijiang District, Leishan County, Guizhou

In the mountainous regions of southern China, villages and towns are often built vertically, tier upon tier climbing up the hillsides to form a picturesque and elegant whole. Qianjiazhai is a hilly village of the Dong nationality, where buildings are all of pile-supported type with gable-and-hipped roof, or overhung gable roof constructed of tile or bark in a plain and unique style. Every house possesses a fireplace. An interesting feature is the line of bamboo tubes, referred to as "distribution of spring water through bamboo pipes", running over a distance of several km and supplying each dwelling with spring water.

Jinjianglou in Jinjiang Village, Shentu Town, Zhangpu County, Fujian

It is divided into three rings. The innermost ring is the tallest and of three stories and was built in the 56th year of the reign of Qianlong (1791 AC). The middle ring is two-storeyed and was built in the 8th year in the reign of Jiaqing (1803 AC). The outermost ring is of one storey, built even later. There is a lookout tower on the front of Jinjianglou and is a story higher the building. So, as viewed from the front, Jinjianglou shows an extremely strong feeling of defense.

vernacular dwellings of the ganlan type in Yunnan belong to this class. Small shops and workshops along urban streets, with a narrow shop front, also have this longitudinal rectangular form, with the room on the street being the shop or workshop, and the wing room at the rear. In rural areas, especially in Jiangnan (south of the Yangtze), vernacular dwellings are often of longitudinal rectangular layout. In spite of the fact that they have weaknesses as regards ventilation and light, they are rather compact and practical. However, such a layout is poorly suited to the life-style of the patriarchal clan society, so it is limited to small dwellings.

3. The L-shaped Plan

The L-shaped plan is also used for small dwellings. Evidence that the L-shaped plan had already been in use at the Han Dynasty was found on an ancient pictorial stone in Ji'nan. There are two versions of the L-shaped plan: the closed and the non-closed, the former being enclosed all round. There are

Plan of Vernacular Dwellings

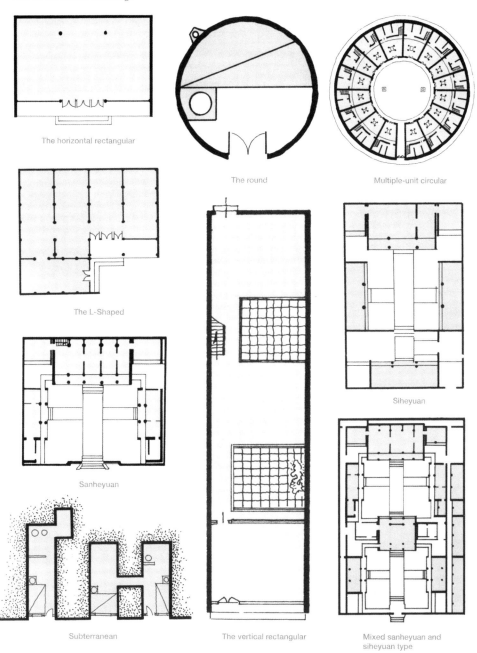

The horizontal rectangular

The round

Multiple-unit circular

The L-Shaped

Siheyuan

Sanheyuan

Subterranean

The vertical rectangular

Mixed sanheyuan and
siheyuan type

many variations on the same theme and these dwellings were free of usual rules and regulations; an example of the phenomenon that the lower down the economic stratum the user was of, the less influence the patriarchal clan system had.

4. The Circular Plan

Circular plans were also used for small dwellings, lending the whole an atmosphere of lightness and vitality. Circular plan layouts are mostly to be found in the southeast of Inner Mongolia, and no doubt originate, as far as the form is concerned, from the Mongolian yurt. The entrances generally face south and there are only one or two small windows in the wall. The layout and outer appearance are very similar to the yurt. The earth kang occupies almost half of the interior space. There is a small oven beside the Kang for cooking and

Sunk Type Cave Dwelling in Henan

Traditional buildings in China are mostly of heavy timber construction in form with relatively monotonous shape of roofing. The sunk type cave dwelling is of an architectural form extremely rare in the world. As a legacy of civilization, it is very valuable. The advantages of subterranean buildings are that it is not necessary to renew the roof 10 to 15 years and that it is not necessary to take consideration of attacking by wind, frost, rain or snow. It has very good fire or earthquake resistance, and even resistance to the harm of radioactive matters to human bodies.

Free-Standing Type Cave Dwelling at No. 37 Xidajie in Mizhi County, Shaanxi
opposite page

The independent type cave dwelling is a vaulted house covered with earth. There are vaulted cave dwellings with unburned earth bricks, and also vaulted cave dwellings of brick vault or stone vault. Such cave dwellings need not rely on a precipice but can stand independently while maintaining advantages of cave dwellings.

heating. Two variants can be found added to this basic layout: one comprising a rectangular room adjacent to the circular one and used for living and cooking; the other consisting of two round rooms connected to the basic circular one, with walls in between and forming thee rooms side by side, each with a separate entrance. Circular plan layouts, though rare, are concise and interesting, possessing their own highly individual features.

5. The Sanheyuan Plan

Courtyard dwellings were appealing on account of their diversity-the zigzagging and meandering of the paths and the rising and falling of the roofs.

The sanheyuan form of layout is very common in rural areas, size and type of dwelling depending on the owner's financial means. Sanheyuan was one

of the basic plans for regular and symmetric dwellings. In western countries, the main building is often exposed, while in China the main building is often enclosed. In western countries, vernacular dwellings are mostly of concentrated layout, while in China, they are set out in multiple courtyards. The multiple courtyard has been used for various types of building in China, the courtyard as such having enjoyed a long history on account of its many advantages.

Though the sanheyuan form of layout is relatively simple in its standard arrangement, there are many variants: (1) the combination of a lateral and a longitudinal sanheyuan; (2) the combination of two sanheyuan arranged to form "H"; (3) the superimposition of two sanheyuan, one wider and one narrower, to form a "凸" shape; (4) the addition of auxiliary buildings around the sanheyuan to form an asymmetric plan.

Almost all the plans of two-, three- or more storied sanheyuan are closed. The buildings of some of them are all storied, but in some cases only the north building is more than just single-storied. Such layouts are mostly to be seen in the south. Closed, the sanheyuan is dramatic, with a variety of corbel gables, other gables and parapets producing a lively and intricate roofscape in contrast to the simplicity of the rectangular structure.

6. The Siheyuan Plan

The view that beauty was to be achieved by wealth was particularly prevalent in the patriarchal clan society of China, and siheyuan form of layout expresses just this combining wealth, rank, luxury and dignified living. With a history of over at least two thousand years, the siheyuan, in the main built by those of solid means, is distributed all over the country and boasts various layouts and facades according to the natural environment and local customs. In scale and content, the siheyuan ranks first among Chinese vernacular dwellings.

The dwellings are symmetrical in plan and have a closed outer appearance. Their form of layout can roughly be divided into two categories: buildings of the first category have their entrance door on the middle axis. Such an arrangement is relatively natural and found mainly in areas south of Huaihe and Northeast China. In the second category, entrance doors are located in the southeast, northeast or northeast corners. Such a configuration is spread throughout such provinces as Shandong, Shanxi, Henan, Shaanxi, etc. and was influenced by Fengshui doctrine of the northern school, which maintained that dwellings should not, like palaces or temples, have their principal gate to

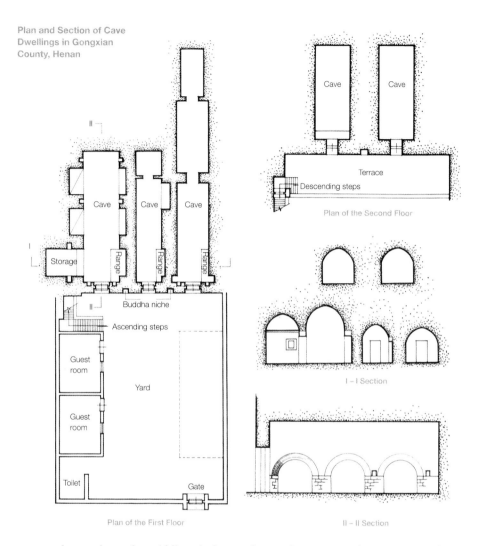

Plan and Section of Cave Dwellings in Gongxian County, Henan

Cave | Cave

Terrace

Descending steps

Plan of the Second Floor

Cave | Cave | Cave

Storage | Range | Range | Range

Buddha niche

Ascending steps

Guest room

Yard

Guest room

Toilet | Gate

Plan of the First Floor

I – I Section

II – II Section

the south on the middle axis, but at the southeast or northwest corner of the building to the south of the road in order to conform with the xiantianbagua (the Eight Diagrams). The reason is that the northwest belongs to gen, which is related to mountains, the southeast to ze, which is related to water. The locating of gate according to such a system led to shan ze tong qi (mountains and water communicating). The northeast belong to zhen, related to thunder. Such a location came second to the above, but the gate could be located here if necessary. However, the southwest belongs to shun which is related to the wind. This was considered an unlucky location and was to be avoided for the gate. Latrines were to be found there. In China, combined layouts are basically highly expressive, their visual effect attractive. Thought is given to how different lengths and widths can be combined, to the juxtaposition of tall and low buildings, to the interlacing and combination of courts and corridors and the location of doors and gates and their interrelation. Complete philosophies of scholarly thought formed the basis far such considerations.

7. The Mixed Sanheyuan and Siheyuan Layout

"Haw deep are the deep, deep parts", a line of an ancient poem makes as reflect upon the spatial effects created by a series of buildings arranged cascade-like within a given space. A mixed arrangement of sanheyuan and siheyuan was by far the best way of creating the illusion of much greater space and depth. This type of plan was used for large dwellings, and comprised various sanheyuan and siheyuan layouts. The garden, the ancestral hall and the library were drawn into the whole, often forming a zigzag pattern and varying in sequence. The beautiful visual effects of such spatial arrangements are immediately apparent.

8. The Ring-Type Plan

At first sight, such layouts have the appearance of a stadium, and they are indeed similar in plan to the ancient Roman arenas. Such ring-typed plans are to be found in southern and western Fujian. They chiefly come in two forms, the first being the unit-type plan. It generally has one ring encircling another. The layout is divided into sector units, one or two dozen in number. Between the rings is a small court. The second version has an interior through corridor, and is not divided into units, there being only individual rooms of the same size. The latter plan again has two variants: the building with a single ring has an open count at the center. There are also versions with the interior through corridor consisting of two or three concentric rings. The largest one has a hall at the center of what is thus a three-ring building. Ring-type layouts are among the most unusual and bizarre forms of building in China.

9. The Cavern Plan

Cavern dwellings are mainly to be found in the provinces of Henan, Shanxi, Shaanxi and Gansu. In these areas, there is little rainwater, timber is lacking and the loess stratum can be up to 300 m thick. There are five forms of layout, namely the "王" form, the "H" form , the "+" form and the "-" form. In the sunkcaverns, there are even courts, and some even have the siheyuan form. It is a hermetic style of life the inhabitants of such dwellings lead, and the caverns resembling flowers in the gullies of vast plateau.

Summing up, the individual vernacular dwelling in China is basically simple in layout. It is the combination of different buildings that is highly varied, producing many complicated forms of arrangement. Particularly the unique and bizarre ring-type layout evokes in the onlooker a sense of profound wonder.

II. A Combination of Forms

There have, since ancient times, been numerous types of vernacular dwellings in China, a vast, multinational country whose topography and climate pose many a problem. "Customs differ just three li away, regulations change a ten li away." The patriarchal clan, geometry and local customs as well as climate, geographical conditions and ethnic characteristics have all played a part in the design of vernacular dwellings, and produced totally different forms.

A Side Veranda Type Dwelling of Korean Nationality in Longjing County, Yanbian Prefecture, Jilin

Veranda boards are found on the front of dwellings of Korean nationality. The origin of veranda boards may be traced back to ancient Chinese buildings. In building palaces, small short columns were often used as bases of platforms. The use of groups of small short columns as bases of platforms or foundations can facilitate venting and prevent from moisture. The outer appearances of dwellings of Korean nationality are very elegant. The main roofs are with gentle slopes, the houses are low, so there is not any feeling of sudden rise and fall.

1.Vernacular Dwellings in Northeast China

The climate in Northeast China can be severely cold, so that vernacular dwellings are often positioned to receive as much sunlight as possible. In front of the main building, there is often a large court to catch more sun. Such vernacular dwellings have strong local features making them different from dwellings inside Shanhaiguan. Particularly on winter days, when the sky is snowy white and the endless snow covered land takes on a slightly blue hue , such dwellings, with their blazing stove fires, offer a blissful retreat from the cold.

Flat roofs are commonly used for the vernacular dwellings of this part of China. Rafters are laid over the beams, which are then covered by daubed straw or soughum stalls, covered in turn by alkaline earth, lime soil etc. Parapets are sometimes added to three sides of the roof, and part of a small pitched roof at front projects forward like the head of a tiger, hence the name hutoufang (tigerhead house).

Adapted to withstand the strong winds indigenous of the area, such dwellings are a good example of the artistic results of such procedures, as well as of the desire of well-to-do families to embellish their homes. The parapets are often decorated with a variety of latticework and fine patterning, and the buildings have an elegant and harmonious look about them.

The Koreans have for generations lived in the border area at the foot of the towering Changbai Mountain, earning their living from the cultivation of the expansive paddy fields. The style of the Korean vernacular dwellings dates back to before the Tang Dynasty, and is similar to vernacular dwellings in Japan.

Roofs are often of the four-pitch type and each house has a porch in front of it where footwear is discarded prior to entering the house. The one room serves both as a sitting room in the daytime and a bedroom at night, and the whole room can be used for sitting or lying. Here, an impression can be gained of the custom of sitting cross-legged, which prevailed in pre-Tang period. With thick brick walls or walls of unfired brick as protection against the bitter cold, the houses of the Koreans have a large fireplace and thin walls that in summer allow the warmth to penetrate more easily. The majority of these dwellings have no courts or encircling walls and social interchange among neighbours is as in a family.

2. Vernacular Dwellings in Jiangsu and Zhejiang

In contrast to the commodious vernacular dwellings in Northeast China, those in Jiangsu and Zhejiang are compact. Northern Zhejiang and southern Jiangsu take in the valley of Lake Tai. The climate is warm and humid, and although neither winter nor summer is extreme, the season of successive rain is relatively long. Houses mostly face south or southeast. Wooden frames are used for load bearing, and the building are well-ventilated, and also well- insulated against the heat of summer, due to their high ridges and generous depth. As far as the layout is concerned, the majority of vernacular dwellings have a small patio and windows with low sills or long partition boards both at front and back.

Both varied in form and of high quality as regards decoration and layout, the vernacular dwellings in this region are usually not enclosed, allowing greater freedom as far as layout and the construction of facades are concerned. As in other areas, the houses of better-off families, have symmetric plan layouts, high enclosing walls, gardens and ancestral halls, resulting in complicated and ambitious layouts with sections of varying importance and character. Regular beam frames are used in wooden frame structures. Buildings are large, built, as far as possible, of high-quality materials and enriched by luxurious ornamental details. Particularly noticeable are the fine treatment of edges and corners and the excellent quality of construction in general.

A view of the Yangtze River from the south from the vantage point of a bridge give a good indication of the prosperity of a town. The rippling reflections of the elegant waterside buildings and the small bridges crossing the slow-flowing river give the whole a quiet and contented atmosphere.

Vernacular dwellings in this region not only have an elegant outer

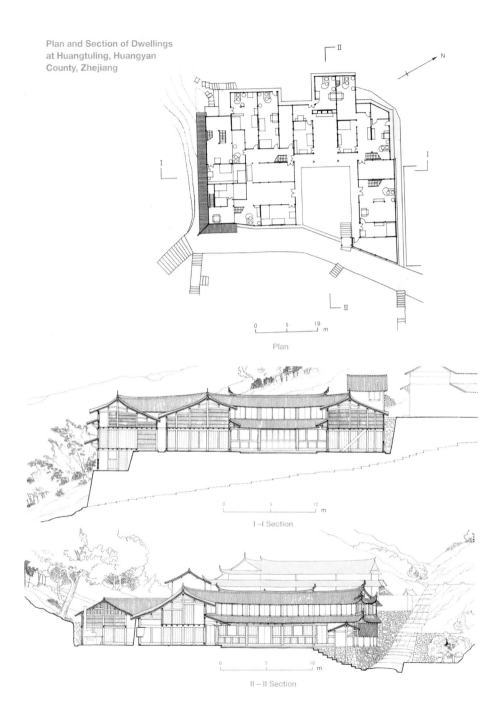

Plan and Section of Dwellings
at Huangtuling, Huangyan
County, Zhejiang

N

0 5 10
m

Plan

0 5 10
m

I –I Section

0 5 10
m

II – II Section

appearance, but impress, too, by the quality and spatial composition of the interior. Interior walls are partitioned, allowing indoor space to be fully utilized. The prosperity and high cultural standards of Jiangsu and Zhejiang have led vernacular buildings being built of elegance, taste and harmony.

3. Vernacular Dwellings in Fujian

Fujian lies in the hilly region of Southeast China. It is a warm and humid mountainous area, cut through by deep valleys and rendered green by dense forests of pine, Chinese fir, cypress and camphor trees. Conditions are therefore favorable for building, and Xuanshan (overhung gable-end) roofs are widely used for vernacular dwellings. At the joint between zhengfang and erfang, perpendicular in layout, italic stepped descending joints (i.e. the mode of the "eagle" joining) are used, elaborate and flexible in design. Fire-sealing gables in vernacular dwellings in Fujian are varied, and italic combinations of xuanshan roofs and fire-sealing gables in particular, each different, are unique.

Vernacular dwellings in Fujian, for example those to be seen between

Umbrella Building in Gaoche Township of Hua'an County, Fujian

The Umbrella Building is located on a hill of 900 m in elevation. It looks like an umbrella as viewed from below, hence the name. There are two rings in the building. Both the inner and the outer rings are of two storeys, but the contour lines of the buildings are different. The inner building is on the top of the hill thus having a higher foundation, while the outer ring surrounds the slope of the hill thus having a lower foundation. Its roof is of the form of broad eaves soffit board.

Fuzhou and Xiamen, stand out on account of their size, variety and fine details. Noticeable, too, is the fact that they possess many of the characteristics of the Song Dynasty curved roof, there being very few straight lines.

From the central bays on, the subcentral bays and the end bays have their eaves successively raised. In the juzhe (raising-and-depression) of the slopes of roofs, each step upwards is progressive, forming concave circular arcs, of rich variety.

In large vernacular dwellings in Fujian, the handling of groups of buildings in courtyards is particularly refined. The courtyard in front of the main building is the largest, the others being smaller to symbolize different categories of precedence. Much attention is paid to the shapes of courtyards to achieve variation and contrast, with square, longitudinal and lateral shapes being interlaced and partitioned. If conditions allow, the floors of courtyard buildings are sloped upwards from front to rear to add dignity, and buildings of the same group are sometimes joined in several sections if it is impossible to link them up on a straight axis due to topological or other reasons.

The most characteristic buildings in vernacular dwellings in Fujian are the earth storeyed buildings, square earth storeyed buildings to be found in the mountainous area of Yongding County in the southwestern corner of Fujian adjacent to Gangdong Province. Some are also to be seen in the counties of Nanjing and Longyan. The way the earth storeyed buildings were built is closely related to defense. The Hakka people had successively migrated southward since the West Jin Dynasty, moving from the middle reach of the Yellow River to such provinces as Jiangxi, Fujian and Guangdong. In times when state corruption was prevalent and bandits abounded, people scattered in the remote mountainous districts were compelled to live in groups according to clan for collective defense. Thus separate small houses evolved into large buildings for

Eryi Building in Dadi Village of Hua'an County, Fujian

The Eryi Building possesses the following characteristics. The first is its size. The diameter is as large as 73.4 m. The second is its thickness. The thickness of the building on the ground floor reaches 2.5 m. The third is the unit type design. The whole building is divided into 12 units, possessing the advantages of modern dwellings. The fourth has the inner through veranda that is usually a feature of the round building. On the inner side of each floor there is a veranda that may be used as balcony.

close dwelling and later into multi-storied high buildings. Square buildings are divided into wufenglou and ordinary square. A dwelling of the former type is usually composed of three tang and two lou. Three tang are antehall, central hall and the main building located on the main axis running from north to south through the middle. Two lou are two longitudinal rectangular buildings, called hengwu locally. In the case of square earth storeyed buildings, left and right are symmetrical and the technique of a rise of level from front to back is also applied. Preference is also given to a topography sloping upwards from front to back. As far as its external appearance is concerned, the square earth storeyed building appears symmetric when seen from the side, however its profile is asymmetrical and of uneven heights.

Some of the small wufenlou have no hengwu, but there is always a main building of three or four stories with load-bearing earth walls. In the township of Fuling is an outstanding example of the employment of wufenglou to create an attractive urban scene. The clever combination of Xieshan and xuanshan roofs, the interlacing of courtyards, the scattered placement of roofs and the use of those with nine ridges and large projecting eaves for special effect, create a setting that the brilliance of its artistry must be considered a masterpiece. Typical characteristics of such building are regular configuration, orderly arrangement, distinction between major and minor sections and a general harmony.

The simplest square is "口" in shape, the most complex of which in external design is those with four storeyes and subsidiary buildings and parlors called cuo locally that are usually only single storeyed. The entrance is located on the central axis. Located precisely at the centre of the subsidiary buildings, just where the entrance gate stands, is a zutang for worshiping one's ancestors. In front of zutang is the hall, and in front of this again is where the ceremony of welcoming guests is performed.

Square earth storeyed buildings are dramatic in appearance. Roof heights are varied and the rugged external appearance of the earth walls makes each look like some wondrous castle.

Even more dramatic are the ring-formed earth storeyed buildings. As we now know, there are six circular buildings measuring over 70 m in diameter as well as the Longjianlou in the township of Jinfeng in the county of Pinghe with a diameter of over 80 m and the Ruxinglou in the county of Yongding with a diameter of only 11 m. There are also circular earth storeyed buildings with layouts that are oval in plan.

Among the unit type circular earth storeyed buildings, the most outstanding is Eryilou in the village of Dadi in the township of Xiandu in Hua'an County. It was built in the 35th year of the reign of Qianlong (1770) and has a diameter of 73.4 m. It is encircled by four rings. It has an outer wall 2.5 m thick at ground level, making it a storied building with the thickest walling. The whole building is divided into 12 units partitioned with fire walls.

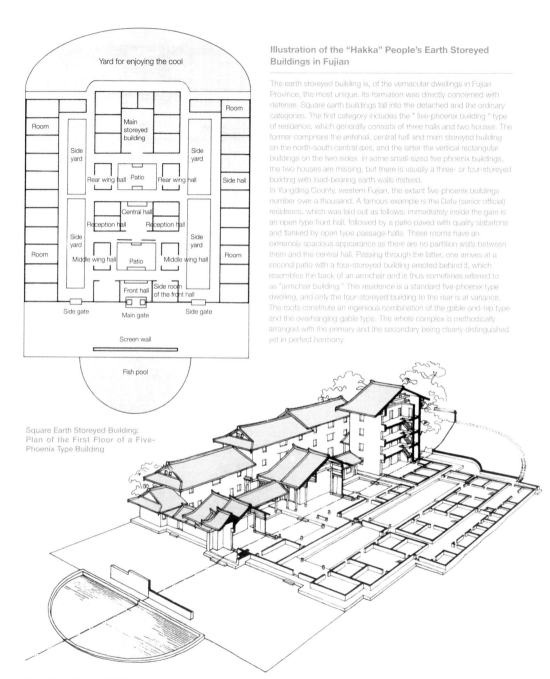

Yard for enjoying the cool

| Room | | | | Room |

Room

Main storeyed building

Side yard

Side yard

Rear wing hall   Patio   Rear wing hall   Side hall

Central hall

Reception hall   Reception hall

Side yard

Side yard

Room

Middle wing hall   Patio   Middle wing hall   Room

Front hall   Side room of the front hall

Side gate   Main gate   Side gate

Screen wall

Fish pool

Illustration of the "Hakka" People's Earth Storeyed Buildings in Fujian

The earth storeyed building is, of the vernacular dwellings in Fujian Province, the most unique. Its formation was directly concerned with defense. Square earth buildings fall into the detached and the ordinary categories. The first category includes the " five-phoenix building " type of residence, which generally consists of three halls and two houses. The former comprises the antehall, central hall and main storeyed building on the north-south central axis, and the latter the vertical rectangular buildings on the two sides. In some small-sized five phoenix buildings, the two houses are missing, but there is usually a three- or four-storeyed building with load-bearing earth walls instead.

In Yongding County, western Fujian, the extant five-phoenix buildings number over a thousand. A famous example is the Dafu (senior official) residence, which was laid out as follows: immediately inside the gate is an open type front hall, followed by a patio paved with quality slabstone and flanked by open type passage-halls. These rooms have an extremely spacious appearance as there are no partition walls between them and the central hall. Passing through the latter, one arrives at a second patio with a four-storeyed building erected behind it, which resembles the back of an armchair and is thus sometimes referred to as "armchair building." This residence is a standard five-phoenix type dwelling, and only the four-storeyed building to the rear is at variance. The roofs constitute an ingenious combination of the gable-and-hip type and the overhanging gable type. The whole complex is methodically arranged with the primary and the secondary being clearly distinguished yet in perfect harmony.

Square Earth Storeyed Building:
Plan of the First Floor of a Five-Phoenix Type Building

Square Earth Storeyed Building:
Cutaway Drawing of a Five-Phoenix Type Building (the Dafu Residence)

An example of the circular earth storeyed building (round buildings) in Fujian is the Chengqi Building in Gaobei Village, Guzhou Township, Yongding County, western Fujian, which is also typical of the fortified round compound in four circles. It was first contructed in the 48th year of the Kangxi reign (AC 1709) and is located within the "Hakka" territory with its dense earth storeyed buildings.

This building complex takes the form of four rings of houses enclosing each other round a centre. Measuring 73m in diameter and with an outer wall circumference of 1,915.6m. It occupies an area of 5,376.17 m2, the first outermost ring consists of four floors totaling 12.4 m in height, each having 72 rooms; the second ring, two floors with 40 rooms each; the third ring single-storeyed, and containing 32 rooms. The fourth, central ring, is an ancestral hall, serving also as a place for meeting, wedding and funeral ceremonies and other public activities. Altogether there are 400 rooms, four staircases and three wells. In the outermost ring, each floorhas an open corridor about one metre wide, and each set of rooms has a kitchen and a dining room on the first floor, storerooms on the second, and living and bedroom on the third and fourth.

The outer wall is built of rammed earth, a thickness of over one metre and has a long-bearing function. It is combined with interior timber frames, and partition walls are added perpendicularly to it. On its level top, a huge circular double-pitch roof has protruding eaves of four metres. For safety reasons, no windows were inserted into the lower part of this wall, and the building possesses a fortress-like character, solid and magnificent.

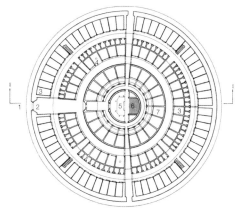

Circular Earth Storeyed Building:
Plan of the Chengqi Building

1. Entrance
2. Entrance hall
3. Kitchen
4. Well
5. Patio
6. Ancestral hall
7. Reception hall
8. Bedroom
9. Storeroom
10. Open corridor

I – I Section

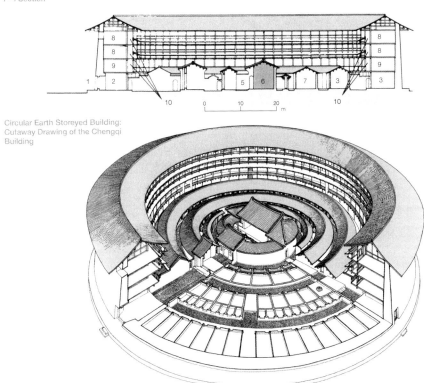

Circular Earth Storeyed Building:
Cutaway Drawing of the Chengqi Building

Vernacular Dwellings in Fenghuang County, Hunan

Balanced beauty and harmonic beauty are a static state of beauty of classic type, while distorted beauty and fragmented beauty are a dynamic state of beauty of modern type. Distorted beauty and fragmented beauty can quickly catch the eye and render a strong impression. The vernacular dwelling in the photo is balanced, uniform and harmonious on the whole, but in detailed technique, emphasis is given to stone built bank. So, it possesses a balanced, and stable classic beauty while shows a prominent, exaggerated, and pragmatic modern beauty.

Of the circular earth storeyed buildings with inner through galleries, the most famous is Chengqilou in the village of Gaobei in Guzhu Township, Yongding County. This circular earth storeyed building was built in the reign of Kangxi of Qing Dynasty (1662~1722). It has a diameter of 73 m and is encircled by four rings, making it very rare. The outermost ring has 72 rooms on each story and four common staircases. The second ring has 40 rooms. The third ring is single-storied with 32 rooms. The building at the center is a zutang.

4. Vernacular Dwellings in Hunan, Hubei and Jiangxi

Vernacular dwellings in Hunan, Hubei and Jiangxi are mostly of wooden structure with tile roofs, and some even with multiple eaves. Tall and of generous size, buildings always have a double-pitch roof with the load borne by

Vernacular Dwellings in Jingde Town, Jiangxi

This group of vernacular dwellings lays stress on the flying motion of eaves of houses and walls to produce an advancing effect and break up the sense of stability of many horizontal lines. Furthermore, upturned roof corners of houses produce a lingering charm of leisure and remoteness, with an artistic effect of floating in the air.

traverse structures and purlins mounted longitudinally.

Vernacular dwellings in these regions vary greatly, but commonly to be found is the type, similar to that such dwellings in southern Anhui, whereby fire-sealing gables or parapets characterize the upper level, screening the roof and lending the architecture a square external appearance. The upper part of the outside walls is treated in a variety of different ways. Buildings are arranged along the outer wall, and include single and multi-storied dwellings. They enclose groups of houses with small courtyards inside. Because rainwater is caught inside the building, this type of residence is called sishuiguitang (water from all sides directed towards the building), implying that such a beneficial commodity is made full use of. Another type has high fire-sealing walls on both sides of the roof, while no parapet is used to expose the gable roof. Fire-sealing walls are found each two or three bays. Such walls have many forms, giving the impression of a series of white overlapping curtains when several vernacular dwellings are combined, and particularly striking when contrasted with dark roofs. There is another category of vernacular dwelling like that in Sichuan, employing overhanging eaves but without a wall and pronounced xuanshan structure. The through jointed wooden structures are totally exposed on the gables.

There are often earth, brick or clay walls with interlaced bamboo filled in the wooden structures, and the external side white-washed. These are features that harmonize well with the dark wooden frame body of the building and give the whole a simple and unpretentious appearance.

Compactness of layout and high density particularly in towns characterize vernacular building in these regions. The "Poem about Hankou" writen by Ye Tiaoyuan in the Qing Dynasty describes in detail the urban density to be found in this area: "Magnificent residences and poor houses are as dense as the forest. It is said that a square inch of land is worth a ton of gold. The main buildings are high and courtyards are small. Nine out of ten houses face south but can receive no sunshine."

Vernacular dwellings so closely-knit hardly allow the overall outer appearance to manifest itself, so emphasis is laid on fire-sealing walls and parapets for ornament. Entrance gates on facades are only decorated at the circumference. Typical for dwellings in mountainous areas are the many types of suspended houses at the upper end of the entrance doors. The simple dwellings located along riversides or set against mountains are supported by tall and slender columns of Chinese fir, resembling the light and smooth lines in a painting with heavy touches of thick ink added.

5. Vernacular Dwellings in Southern Anhui

Southern Anhui was called Huizhou in ancient times. In the Ming and Qing dynasties, the rich merchants of Huizhou, having made their fortune in other places, often returned to their place of birth and built houses. There are many ancient well-kept vernacular dwellings of unique style still extant. They are often two-or three-storied and are 口 or 目 shaped. The outer wall of the house is, apart from the entrance, only broken by several small windows, which are either carved or variously decorated by ground bricks or black bluestone, standing in marked contrast to the plain white walls.

Vernacular dwellings in Huizhou during the Ming and Qing dynasties were all large buildings, and of these the sanheyuan and the siheyuan were the most common. High walls were used inside the courtyard to divide into small patios. On both sides of the antecourt are wing rooms. The central on the ground floor is the main room and the rooms to the left and right serve as bedrooms. Partition boards are usually not used in the main room, which is of the open type. The wing rooms are generally relatively small with regard to the bays and shallow in depth to give more daylight. For the higher floors, the form known as "horse racing building" (storied buildings forming a square with a ringed verandah built along the inner sides) is usually adopted, the through verandah encircles the building and fine carved partition boards taking the form of wooden balustrades are used for ornament.

The study and boudoir are located upstairs both for privacy and the view, the beauty of which could provide enjoyment or give spiritual consolation in times of need. On some of the second floors, a small window was set inside the carved balustrade so that the young unmarried ladies of the house could have a surreptitious peep to see whether the young man just visiting was a suitable match.

The outer hollow walls of vernacular dwellings have file sheathing. As wooden columns and not the walls were used for load-bearing, hollow walls were chosen for insulating purposes. Rich families, would have decorative wooden panels installed on the inner side of the outer walls as a precaution against thieves, who would wet walls at night, cut through the lime seam with bamboo blades and remove the bricks one by one to form a hole through which they could enter the house.

Further precautions taken by well-to do families were the installation of concealed rooms, the entrances to which were often hidden by a brick wall, carved wooden ornament etc., and sandwich design, whereby cavities were left between the floorboards of the upper story and the ceiling of the ground floor and used for hiding the family's gold, silver and jewellery. Old trees, clear brooks, paved roads, square pavilions and small bridges are typical features of the villages in Southern Anhui. Stout and bulky old trees and dense, dark green woods form the setting for the ancient wayside pavilions, houses and paifang (archway, a decorated entrance with arch erected in front of a group of buildings at the access to a city sector or at an important road junction).

The brick carving applied in the vernacular dwellings of the region deserves special mention. From the technical and compositional point of view, brick carving during the Ming Dynasty was somewhat plain and naive. It could, however, in the Qing Dynasty be exquisite. Inspired by the means of expression employed by the painters of vertical and hand scrolls, the brick carvers produced wonderfully carved pieces, paying particular attention to plot and composition and the effects that could be achieved by successively engraving more deeply.

Interestingly, it was only for a very short period, namely that stretching from the middle to the late Ming Dynasty, that the art of vernacular dwellings in south Anhui flourished. Its rise and decline was synchronous with that of the local Xin'an school of painting and the Anhui woodcut school, reflecting the local economic and cultural conditions, the creative level of artists and masters and the interest people took in art at the time.

6. Vernacular Dwellings in Guangdong

Materials used in traditional vernacular dwellings are simple, mostly earth and wood. War, fire, natural calamities and the rainy climate have all taken their

A Small Lane by a Residence in Nanhua Township, Meixian County, Guangdong

Materials used in traditional vernacular dwellings are simple, mostly earth and wood. War, fire, natural calamities and the rainy climate have all taken their toll, and as a result, there are very few old vernacular dwellings still extant. Guangdong is the province with the highest population of overseas emigrants. Usually emigrant Chinese returned to their native places for purchasing field and building house. So vernacular dwellings there often reflect the influence of forms of foreign architecture and some of exotic structural members.

Dihua Building, Songkou Township, Meixian County, Guangdong

Dihua Building belongs to the vernacular dwelling of Hakkas in northern Guangdong. Its basic form is like a lock (because the layout of the house is like an ancient lock). The lock dwelling is a kind of independent transverse house, composed of a vestibule and a kitchen at two ends. The enclosing wall is on the opposite sides to form a separate rectangular courtyard. When several such houses are arranged in parallel, the houses added between them are called lateral houses. There are buildings of three lateral and four houses. The Dihua Building is a two-storeyed building of six lateral houses.

toll, and are only very few vernacular dwellings built prior to the Ming dynasty still extant, an exception being Xu's residence in Chaozhou.

One type of vernacular dwelling in Guangdong was the parallel one, uniting several households. As dwellings built with earth walls could neither withstand the frequent strong winds nor were easy to defend, the parallel type was adopted, which was more ideal.

Zhutongwu (a bamboo tube house), also called Zhougancuo, is a type of building often found in the towns of Guangdong. The facade is single-bay, but the building is of generous depth. The lobby, the kitchen, the sitting room, the study, and the bedrooms are often single bay in several rows with small courtyards in-between. The form of layout is narrow that it could be compared to the stem of the bamboo. A block comprises a dozen or so zhutongwu parallel to each other and with rear doors as well. Members of the same family owning several Zhougancuo would open a side door between two courtyards. The rooms of such dwellings follow on from each other on a straight axis.

Another type of unique dwelling in Guangdong is the Diaolou, of which

only around 1400 still exist in the county of Kaiping. The earliest Diaolou is
a three-storied Diaolou in the village of Ying still in existence in the Chikan
District of Kaiping County. It bears the name of Yinglonglou. According to
the records of the county, its history goes back more than three hundred years.
Diaolou like strongholds, have thick outer walls and are as high as blockhouses,
and provide excellent defence if attacked by bandits or floods occur.

Unique too, in the mountainous border area of Fujian, Guangdong and
Jiangxi, is the castle-type vernacular dwelling, the weiwu of the Hakka people,
a branch of the Han, who migrated from the north and speak a special dialect.
Weiwu differ from the earth storeyed buildings in Fujian in the following ways.
Firstly, the weiwu is mostly built of brick and stone. Secondly, weiwu consist of
individual encircling buildings of a single story or several stories and are thus
groups of buildings but not buildings in themselves. Weiwu in Shixing County
in Guangdong are splendid examples of this type. "No village has no weiwu,
without weiwu a village cannot be a village." Generally, weiwu are curved,
oval, or square in shape with very high enclosing walls and rather awe-inspiring.
Weiwu are classified by local people into several types such as weilongwu,

sidianjin, zoumalou, wufenglou and diantangshi. Of these, the weiwu built in the Qing Dynasty in the village of Mantang, Aizi Town - Dawei, deserve their reputation as the most impressive weiwu in Northern Guangdong.

Vernacular dwellings in Guangdong are rarely limited by traditional rules and regulations, and have thus been able to lead the way in the making of modern residences out of traditional vernacular dwellings.

7. Vernacular Dwellings in Shanxi and Shaanxi

The valley of the Huanghe River, with its clement climate and plentiful supply of water, was once fertile. The following lines taken from Shijing, a book of the poetry of ancient China, attest to this. "Look into the forest, there are many deer." "On the slope, there are varnish trees", in the swamps, there are chestnut trees." "On the slope, there are mulberry trees; in the swamps, there are poplar trees." Conditions, alas, have changed; wars and the destruction caused by man have left their mark.

Since the Ming Dynasty, many natives of Shanxi have earned their living in other places, but on becoming rich and returning to their native land, they transformed the place into a region famous for its thriving economy.

The arrangement of vernacular dwellings in Shanxi and Shaanxi is comparatively compact narrow courtyards being chosen as protection against sand blown by the wind, and there are corridors in the main house and wing houses in courtyards. Large country residences are often equipped with small square brick lookout towers called kanjialou. Roofs are of the gable-roof type. There are often handsome colored paintings and engravings on the efang (architrave, tie-beam between two peripheral columns, supporting maybe one or more intermediate bracket sets in buildings with a dougong.

In Shanxi, vernacular dwellings of the cave-house type are often to be found, with brick arching under flat roofing (i.e. independent cave-house). In the case of well-to-do families, such dwellings were obviously not chosen for economic reasons but for the advantages they offered; warm in winter, cool in summer and the protection the thick walls gave when fire broke out or in the event of attacks by robbers. In the case of ordinary families with limited financial means, main houses were built as independent cave dwellings, while the wing houses are dwellings with a single-sided pitched roof. In spite of their age, the elegant style of such dwellings can still be perceived. Tasteful, too, are the latticework on the doors and windows and the colour of the moire on the beam-ends.

Ordinary families again around Shanxi often live in sanheyuan or siheyuan consisting of houses with a one-sided pitched roofs. All the roofs are inclined toward the courtyard even the entrance gate and the daozuo (a room lying on the principal axis of a building and opposite the main room, i. e. Usually facing north have a one-sided pitched roof inclining inwardly). With roofs inclining inward, the outer walls of the building seem very high, offering a sense of safety.

In such type of dwellings, walls are of rammed earth. In order to protect them from erosion caused by rainwater, two rows of thin tiles are laid parallel to each other on the upper part of the outer wall and form an integral artistic whole with the roof above. The artistic conception of such dwellings is simple but highly suggestive.

Courtyards in this region are surprisingly narrow and long, running from north to south. Gables of the eastern and western bays shield the east and west rooms of the main building. Courtyards are sometimes less than two meters wide, resembling an indoor corridor in a Western building, except that there is no roof.

The cave-dwelling of Shanxi and Shaanxi is unique in conception, and various shapes exist, depending on the natural environment, geographical features and local customs. They can, however, be divided into three categories as far as the configuration and structure are concerned, namely: the kaoya (against a precipice), the xiachen (sunk down) and the duli (independent) types. Kaoya-type cave-houses are further divided into kaoshan (against a mountain) and yan'gou(facing a gully). Caves are often arranged in curved or zigzag lines, lending them harmonious beauty and architectural artistry. Where the height of the slope permits, cave-dwellings are often arranged in layers like storied houses. Xiachen type cave-dwellings are constructed underground, and mainly distributed in loess areas without slopes or gullies. Construction of such dwellings is as follows: a square pit is first dug out to form a siheyuan, the cave-dwellings then being dug out in the direction of the four walls. Such dwellings are only to be found in China and Tunisia. While in Tunisia, existing cave-dwellings of this type are rare, they are still widely used by a good number of people in China, a fact that is unique in the world. The duli cave-dwelling is a kind of arch-type house covered with earth. There are cave-dwelling both of fired and unfired bricks, earth, and with brick or stone arches. As stated above, such dwellings need not lie against a precipice and can stand independently, but still possess the merits of a cave-house.

Cave-dwellings represented an ideal form of building for the sweeping loess highlands in which they are situated. Warm in winter, cool in summer, taking up very little land and easy to build, they are ideally insulated against fire, wind and noise, even offering protection in the event of an earthquake. A gully can be filled with layers of such dwellings, dwellings that almost dissolve into the natural environment.

8. The Diaofang of Tibetan people

Diaofang is the common form of building on the Qing-Zang Plateau and in some areas of Inner Mongolia. According to *Houhanshu (the history of the Western Han Dynasty)*, it already existed before the 6th year of the Han Dynasty (111 BC). Built of irregular-shaped stones or of earth, the dwellings are of two or three stories, and because they are like a pillbox in outer appearance, they are called diaofang (pillbox house). The name diaofang may be traced back to the reign of Qianlong of the Qing Dynasty. Diaofang of the Tibetan people have an austere and almost sacred look. The walling is thick at the base and thin at the top, with the load borne by the walling, compact rib-work and flat roof.

Schematic Drawings of Tibetan Dwelling in Lhasa City

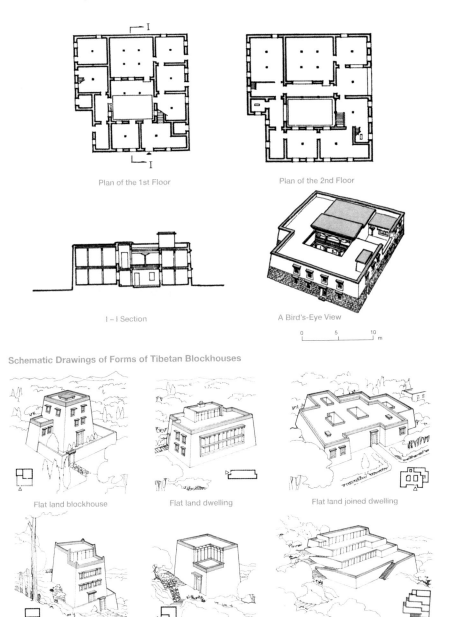

Plan of the 1st Floor

Plan of the 2nd Floor

I – I Section

A Bird's-Eye View

0   5   10
              m

Schematic Drawings of Forms of Tibetan Blockhouses

Flat land blockhouse

Flat land dwelling

Flat land joined dwelling

Mountain blockhouse

Mountain blockhouse

Lamas' residence
in the mountain temple

A Residence in Lhasa,
Tibet

This is a medium-sized
vernacular dwelling located
in a green courtyard. The
house is of stone block wall
and flat roof. Windows
facing south are of large
glass panes (French windows
on the second floor) for
receiving sunshine. White
walls form strong contrast to
black exterior window trims.
The building is luxury and
comfortable, elegant and clear
and appealing.

The general layout is simple and usually square or L-shaped. For topographical and economic reasons, regions such as the Qing-Zang plateau have many undulating mountains and hills, ordinary dwellings are built upwards to conserve land, sometimes having a small courtyard in between. Diaofang have fine and inspiring interiors and an impressive external appearance.

The ground floor is generally used for raising livestock and for the storage of fodder. Floors above consist of sitting rooms, bedrooms, a kitchen and storage space. On the top floor, there is a flat roof for drying, a Buddhist scripture hall, an airing gallery and a toilet. The Buddhist scripture hall is located in the best position, worthy of particular mention, the toilet. Some project out of the wall, supported by extended brackets, and have the enclosure braided with twigs so that the feces drop directly into the manure pit outside the wall.

Vernacular dwellings of Tibetans stand out on account of their successful treatment of profiles. The almost unavoidable monotony of the facades of buildings with a square or L-shaped layout is counteracted by projecting wooden structures, which contrast well with the solid and heavy stone walls and give the whole variety. Attention has not only been paid to function but to the general artistic effect as well.

Plan, Section and Elevation of the Mongolian Yurt and Drawings of its Skeleton Structure

Schematic Drawing of the Skeleton Structure of the Mongolian Yurt

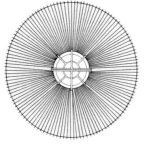

Plan of the roof

Elevation of the skeleton

Schematic drawing of the roof structure

Schematic drawing of the wall network structure

Movable-Style Yurt

Plan

Elevation

Stationary Yurt

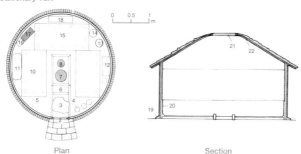

Plan

Section

1. Door
2. Felt
3. Stove
4. Bed-cum-Seat for women
5. Bed-cum-Seat for men
6. Clothes and quilts
7. Bowl shelf
8. Water vat
9. Rice vat
10. Vat
11. The host's red felt-cum-seat
12. Cupboard
13. Case
14. Buddha altar

1. Steps
2. Door
3. Fur
4. Water vat
5. Place for boots
6. Fuel
7. Large fire brazier
8. Fire brazier
9. Felt bed-cum-seat for women
10. Felt bed-cum-seat for men
11. Sheepskin
12. Case
13. Rice vat
14. Vat
15. The host's felt bed-cum-seat
16. Table
17. Buddha altar
18. Suitcase
19. Brick step
20. Felt
21. Skylight
22. Woolen felt roof

9. Mongolian Yurt

The Mongolian yurts are the tradition dwellings of the Mongolians, and were called qionglu in the Han Dynasty. The exterior consists of wool felt stretched over a simple wooden frame, layout and profile both circular in shape, the yurt is an ideal form of dwelling for a nomadic people as the prefabricated parts are constructed in such a way that erecting and taking down the yurt is quick and easy. A stove is placed in the center of the yurt, its chimney protruding out of the top of the tent. Around the stove is an area kept free for sitting and lying. Walling consists of twigs woven into a hind of fencing. Yurts are sometimes even set on a circular fireplace for warmth. Similar felt yurts are also used by other nomadic peoples such as the Kazakh.

10. Vernacular Dwellings in Sichuan

As a result of the climate in the Sichuan Basin with its hot summer, rare snow in winter, its plentiful rainfall and moderate winds, vernacular dwellings are of the single-story type with tile roofs, sihetou, and large overhanging eaves. Attics are used for storage, and help insolate the building.

Vernacular Dwellings in Shangli Town, Ya'an County, Sichuan

As the Sichuan basin is a mountainous region, the houses are constructed in line with local conditions, while the orientation of houses is not given much attention. Courtyards are rather shallow to spare the land used. The roofs of the siheyuan residences are successively overlapped to avoid drenching by rainwater and too much sunshine into the house in summer days. Eaves and overhung gable-end roofs of the house are much projected to prevent earth walls from erosion by rainwater. In the photo shops mostly have the store in the front and workshop in the rear, and the rooms upstairs for living.

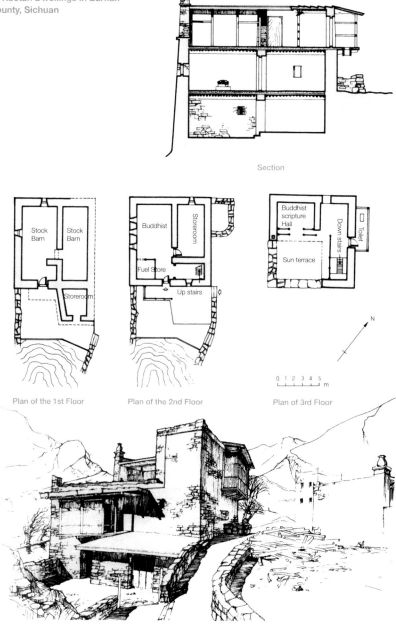

Plan, Section and Perspective
of Tibetan Dwellings in Barkan
County, Sichuan

Section

Stock
Barn

Stock
Barn

Storeroom

Plan of the 1st Floor

Buddhist

Storeroom

Fuel Store

Up stairs

Plan of the 2nd Floor

Buddhist
scripture
Hall

Down stairs

Toilet

Sun terrace

Plan of 3rd Floor

N

0 1 2 3 4 5
m

Perspective

Dwellings in the mountainous regions of Sichuan are built along practical lines. Courtyards are not very deep to save land, roofs in a siheyuan join up to keep out the rain and protect the inside rooms from excessive sunlight in summer. Overhanging eaves and gable-ends project widely to protect walls constructed of earth or wooden panels, or those of the pile and earth type, from damage by rainwater.

The towering suspended houses located among the group of vernacular dwellings at Linjiangmen in Chongqing are a magnificent sight. The alleys are so narrow that they resemble a labyrinth, and at each turn a new and completely different world presents itself. As an old Chinese poem says, "To the end of the way, seemingly blocked by mountains and rivers, there appears a village anew, with thick willows and bright blossom."

Vernacular dwellings in Sichuan are all of the through-jointed frame type. The local people are adept in utilizing the topography. Constriction is carried out according to the actual situation without adhering to established rules and regulations. In one and the same dwelling, there are often several contours on ground level. The Tuitai of the house base are traversal and longitudinal to coordinate the heights of roofs. Eaves are not very high and branches of trees growing in the vicinity result in an attractive combination of architecture and nature. In the vernacular dwellings in Chongqing and the mountainous region of Eastern Sichuan, the orientation of houses is not important and they are built against precipices. Suspended houses are far extended, some at different levels, producing a magnificent and brilliant sight.

11. Siheyuan in Beijing

The size of courtyards in dwellings is related to the climate. The colder the climate, the larger the courtyards will be. The aesthetic function of Chinese architecture is not only to give pleasure by dint of the outer appearance, but also, and even more important to "help and enlighten human relations". The siheyuan is a regular square with straight sides, with an inside configuration of the character "井" implied. Since Jingtianzhi (the system of the 井 –shaped field) of remote antiquity up to mingtang , palace buildings, ancestral temples, the traditional architecture of China has consistently endeavored to give architectural art clear and definite social, political and ethical meaning. Division using the character of "井" gives rise to a centre which implies symmetry, stability, dignity and seriousness. To it, many symbolized contents may be

attributed. According to the bagua (eight diagrams initiated in Yijing (the Book of Changes), Kun indicates the North symbolizing the earth, and qian indicates the South symbolizes Heaven. Orientation to the north and the south therefore means conformance with heaven and earth, while conforming with the natural laws would ensure prosperity and bring luck. Huangdizhaijing (the classical Book on Buildings by Huangdi) reads: "The house is the pivot of yin and yang and the model of human relations. Only sages with wisdom can interpret the principle." In a siheyuan, only the north room was considered ideal for dwelling purposes but it was in fact the halls used for reception and sacrificial rites that were located here, the east and west wing rooms, the dozuo and rear hall being the rooms actually dwelt in. As stated in the Liji (the Book of Rites); "A man of dignity considers the ancestral temples first, the stable and storehouse second and the room for dwelling last when constructing houses." Reason therefore prevails over the function in China. The more sophisticated the configuration of the vernacular dwelling is, the more this maxim holds. The entrance gate, the yingbi, the chuihuamen, and the verandah all add dignity. Spatial arrangement within a siheyuan is orderly and the buildings are of reasonable dimension. In the inner courtyard of a siheyuan in Beijing there are often verandahs weaving round from the second gate to the main house, not only offering protection against rain, but also adding interest to the courtyard as they zigzag their way through.

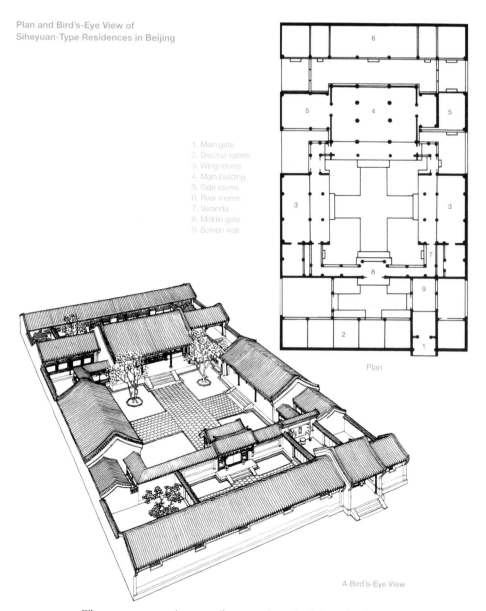

1. Main gate
2. Daozuo rooms
3. Wing rooms
4. Main building
5. Side rooms
6. Rear rooms
7. Veranda
8. Middle gate
9. Screen wall

Plan

A Bird's-Eye View

The entrance gate is generally opened on the left at the front with the zhaobi located immediately inside. The deep courtyard is quiet, and as it cannot be seen from outside, functions as an outdoor living room in summer. Potted plants transform it into a small and idyllic often brick-paved garden.

12. Vernacular Dwellings in Xinjiang

Rainfall in the Turfan Basin in Xinjiang is practically non-existent, with so-called dust-rain falling on spring and summer days. At this time, loess dust is everywhere even cutting out the sunlight. The Uygur people adapt to this climate by planting grapevines and fruit trees in the courtyards of their dwellings and in summer eating outdoors or receiving guests under the grapevine.

Their flat-roofed dwellings are made of adobe and have wooden beam roof with compact rib-work of compactly combined horizontal and vertical ribbed slabs which serve the purpose of partitioning or load-bearing in the same way as beams and posts. The configuration is complicated, flexible and varied. Space is often divided up by adobe floral walls and arched doors. As temperature in this region can rise as high as 47°C, falling at night to just 20°C, walls of buildings are constructed of immature soil and made especially thick. Grapevines are often to be seen forming long corridor along streets, and provide welcome shade.

Although the climate poses no problems for houses built of immature earth, well-to-do families still have their dwellings built of bricks as a precaution against erosion. Fine carvings decorate arched galleries, wall surfaces, niches, fireplaces, the compact ribwork, ceilings, etc. As the inhabitants are Muslim, green colors are mostly used. In dwellings of the common people, internal decorations are simpler, and there is usually little furniture, but beautiful tapestries are hung on the walls for decoration.

An Inner Veranda in the Wufuerji's Residence at Kashi Street, Yining City, Xinjiang

In Yining City there are many residences of Uigur nationality built by craftsmen from Hetian after the 1930s. They bear a very strong Islamic style. Capitals in colonnades are of various forms. Column shafts are carefully carved. Doors and windows, etc. are decorated with colored paintings. Various delicate geometric patterns are used for combination of window muntins. The integrated use of various decorations brings about a brilliant and delicate artistic atmosphere.

Plan and Cutaway View of Uighur Dwellings in Xinjiang

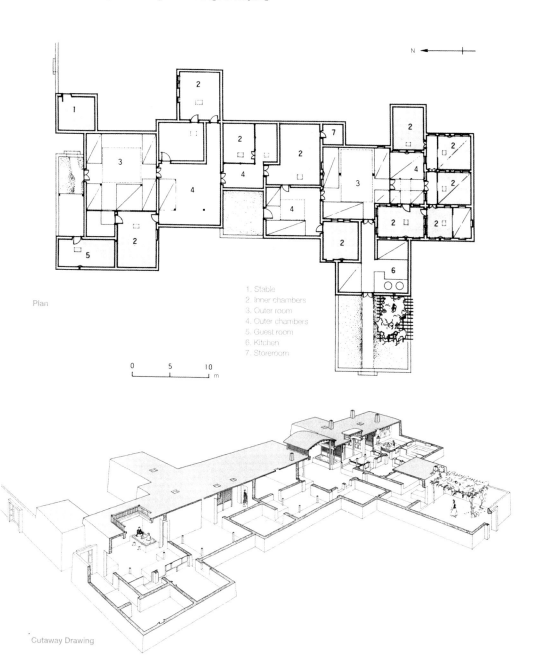

N

Plan

1. Stable
2. Inner chambers
3. Outer room
4. Outer chambers
5. Guest room
6. Kitchen
7. Storeroom

0   5   10
              m

Cutaway Drawing

Vernacular Dwellings in Jinzhu Village, Heping Township, Longsheng County, Guangxi

Some people refer the wooden storeyed building in the upper photo to the pile-supported building. But the true pile-supported building is on a platform supported by piles that are buried in the ground at one end. It can still be found today in some dwellings of the Miao nationality in northern Guangxi. The wood storeyed buildings are generally of three storeys. People live in the upper two floors, whereas livestock is raised in the lower floor. In the whole village, there are many transverse horizontal roads, while longitudinal upward and downward roads are few. There is only one major longitudinal road, which is shown below the wood storeyed building in the lower photo. For the sake of saving land, many vernacular buildings are built over roads.

13. Vernacular Dwellings in Southwest China

The provinces of Yunnan, Guizhou and Guangxi are famous for the uniqueness and beauty of their scenery. The population includes minority ethnic groups such as the Daizu, Jingpo, Dong, Wa, Aini and Shui, and the vernacular dwellings have a variety of different forms, many tribes adopting ganlan-type buildings.

These have a long history. In the period of the Hemudu culture, about 1000 years ago, very mature ganlan-type buildings already existed. The Liao Zhuan, a description of the Liao nationality in the book *Wei Shu*, which tells the history of the Wei Dynasty, says the following, "The Liao nationality is a branch of the Nanman. They live in the area stretching from Hanzhong to Qiong, Ze, Chuan and Dong, and consist of many branches scattered through the valleys... Leaning against trees, they pile up wood to live thereon." Ganlan-type dwellings were small storied buildings with bamboo for the columns or beams, the upper floors for dwelling and the lower ones for raising livestock or storing sundries.

Ganlan-type dwellings can be of the high-storied or the low-storied type depending on the height of the void space of columns and beams on the lower floors. The most common type is three-storied: the uppermost floor being a bedroom, the floor in-between a sitting room and ground floor serving as a pen for animals and storage space.

In sparsely populated areas, ganlan-type dwellings are ideal for fending off wild beasts. They also uphold the ancient tradition of huotang (fireplace, a hollow made in the floor for an open fire for the cooking of food, the heating of water and the drying of clothes). The huotang is also to be found on the second floor, the number depending on the ethnic group and the number of brothers; but there is generally at least one. In addition to the mentioned above, they also serve to repel mosquitoes, and blackened beams and floor panels are less likely to be attacked by woodworm. The huotang is also used for smoking meat and vegetables.

Dwellings of the outer-gallery type of the Jingpo in Yunnan are of the low storied ganlan type. The roofs are double pitch, larger at the top and smaller lower down. Bronze funeral objects unearthed from a tomb with a wooden outer coffin and a bronze inner coffin found in the village of Xiangyun County in Yunnan Province during the period of Warring States (400 BC), testify to the fact that there were already at that time such ganlan-type buildings with roofs of inverted trapezoidal shape with a longer ridge and shorter eaves. In ancient

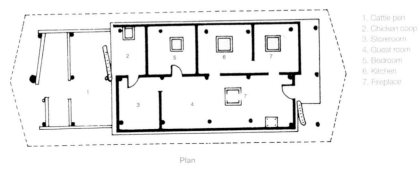

1. Cattle pen
2. Chicken coop
3. Storeroom
4. Guest room
5. Bedroom
6. Kitchen
7. Fireplace

Plan

Schematic Drawings of Jingpo Dwellings (Low-Storeyed Type)

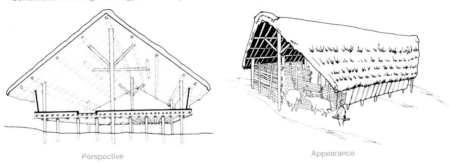

Perspective

Appearance

times, the heads of oxen or even human heads were hung from the eaves as a demonstration of the fighting spirit and courage of the master of the house. The Jingpo still use this form of dwelling.

Jinggan-type dwelling is also a style of building that was already in existence in ancient China. Patterns on vessels for storing shells and bronze articles unearthed from Shizhai Mountain in Yunnan give us an indication of what these dwellings looked like, the method of construction emerging as early as the Han Dynasty. The jinggan-type storied building constructed in the reign of Wudi of the Han Dynasty was very tall, and was once described in the following way: "Climbing only half way up a jinggan-type storied building leaves one feeling faint."

Both the outer and inner walls of jinggan-type dwellings are made of piled-up debarked round or square logs, with deep grooves being provided on the contact surfaces of the logs to facilitate stable piling and water-proofing.

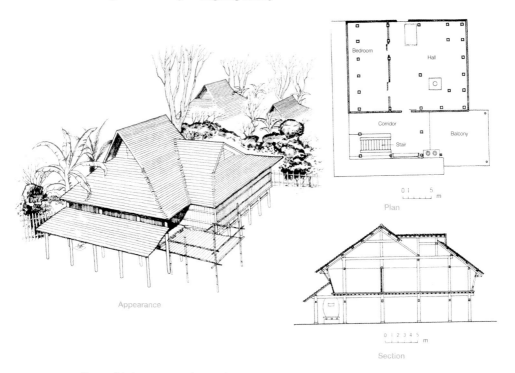

Bedroom

Hall

Corridor

Balcony

Stair

0 1 5 m

Plan

Appearance

0 1 2 3 4 5 m

Section

Crossed joints are used at wall corners. The logs of inner partition walls are also crossed and exposed. Lapping round logs are roughly exposed without being painted. The name of this type of building derives from its shape. The roofs are generally of straw, or bark, but roofs of wood slices are more representative. Jinggan-type dwellings are scattered about in small villages as a precaution against fire. Of these, the most impressive are those of the Naxi in Yongning County, Yunnan.

The city of Dali in the province of Yunnan is a beautiful place, and famous for its folk songs. Eighteen brooks from Cangshan Mountain flow here into lake Erhai. The crystal-clear water is partly diverted through the town, making a murmuring sound as it runs through the stone channels of the streets and alleys. The brooks themselves are rendered green by the waterweeds, swaying like stalks of wheat in the breeze as the water flows gently over them. Bai girls are often to seen washing clothes at dust, an attractive sight against the background of the

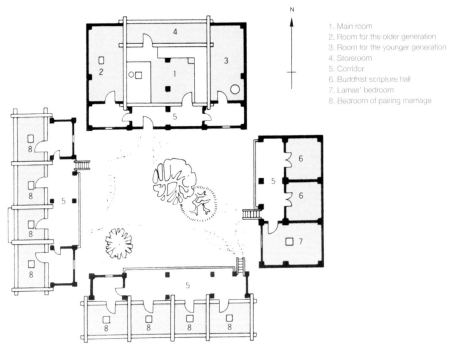

N

1. Main room
2. Room for the older generation
3. Room for the younger generation
4. Storeroom
5. Corridor
6. Buddhist scripture hall
7. Lamas' bedroom
8. Bedroom of pairing marriage

houses with their black tiles and white walls. Bai vernacular dwellings are justly famous. Sanfangyizhaobi and sihewutianjing are the layouts typically used and buildings are built to best withstand the strong gales and frequent earthquakes.

A so-called fang is a two-storied house comprising three bays. Sanfang-yizhaobi is a sanheyuan composed of three encircling two-storied houses of three bays each, plus a zhaobi. Such layouts are relatively common and are the most popular for the vernacular dwellings of the Bai.

Sihewutianjing is a siheyuan plus an entrance zhaobi and the encircling walls to make five large and small tianjing (patio, a small roofless space in a building or in a yard enclosed by houses on four sides or on three sides with a wall on the fourth). The Bai people prefer their houses to be built by the side of a hill or mountain, only thus is the well-being of the family guaranteed. The rear end of the principal axis of the building is thus set against a nearby hill, it being forbidden to have the back of a vernacular building

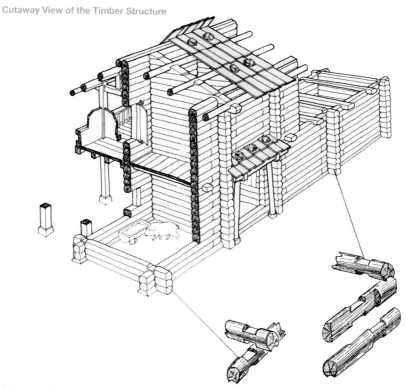

facing a gully or an open place.

Guizhou Province is located to the east of the Yungui Plateau. Here hills rise and fall, surface soil is poor with rocks and stones everywhere. The local people utilize the readily available material to build their houses, and even flat mountain rocks are sometimes used for the walling of vernacular dwellings. The wooden frames of the houses are of the through-jointed type. The sloping roof surfaces are covered with thin layers of limestone and not given ridge tiles, solving the problem of roof ridge leaking.

In many villages, too, the ground is paved with stone slabs, the floors are of stone, water urns are also of stone and mangers are chiseled out of stone blocks. Whole villages of slab houses have a special character. Hundreds of steps zigzag their way upwards to the top of the village. Arched gates span the road and high staggered buildings constructed of flat pieces of stone piled up one on top of the other are an impressive sight. Stone slab houses are to be found around the

Huaxi District of Guiyang, Zhenning and Anshun in the province of Guizhou, in Ankang in the province of Shaanxi and in the mountainous region of the municipality of Beijing. From the famous waterfall in Huangguoshu one can easily walk to the shitouzhai (stone village) in Zhenning.

Yunnan Province is located on the plateau. The climate is spring-like all year round without extremes of heat and cold. Strong winds, however, can blow, so vernacular dwellings have thick earth walls and semi-cylindrical roof tiles. One finds Yikeyin (seal) vernacular dwellings, so called because their form of layout is as square as a seal. The sanjiansi'er yikeyin type is the most common, sanjiansi'er denoting these main central rooms and two rooms on each side.

Seal-Shaped Type Dwelling

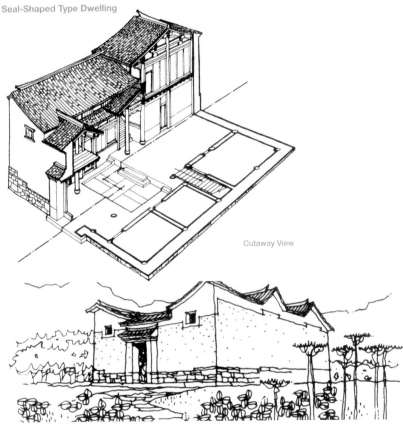

Cutaway View

Appearance

84

Such layouts not only fulfil the functional requirements of living but also those of defence. Yikeyin houses are all multi-storied, with people living upstairs and the ground floor used for livestock and storage. The ground floor of the main house is taken up by the main room, used to receive guests. Rooms to the left and right of the main room serve as bedrooms. The central bay upstairs is used as the family hall for worshipping Buddha. Two or three yiheyin units can be used in line when it is a question of building larger dwellings, and those of high-clan families have a daozuo of daobachi at the entrance.

III. The Layout of Towns and Villages

The layout of towns and villages will be considered here from three aspects: the siting of the town or village, the configuration of streets, and the locating of squares by roads and around pavilions.

1. The Siting of the Town and Village

Siting was generally carried out by a geomancer through milong (seeking for the dragon), chasha (inspecting the sand), Guanshui (observing waters) and dianxue (pointing out the exact location), to ensure that town or village

Water Street in Suzhou, Jiangsu

In the south of the Yangtze River, water systems are well-developed. Boats and ships are the main of transport vehicles. Water streets are formed along rivers. Sotto porticos are often found on both sides of main water streets for sheltering from sunshine and rain. On minor water streets, every house has a private dock built of several stone blocks.

Xinnan Street in the Seat of Shexian County, Anhui

Door openings, flying beams and even bridge galleries are often found at the intersections of small alleys and streets. Such spatial organization gives passers-by a feeling of the space division of the streets. Some small alleys indicate their start with steps, not only solving the problem of difference in elevation, but also stressing the function of the space of small alley. Xinnan Street here, starts with a door opening, then climbs several dozens of steps, and finally ends with a stone memorial archway.

were well located. Such site selection and point location is called xiangdi (land appraising), and is actually an on-the-spot investigation. Once the investigation has been completed, the geomancer encircles the site of the future village and draws the plan of layout. Most common was the sitting of a village with a hill in the background, a hill to screen in the foreground and water encircling. The theory of geomancy mainly uses wuxing (the five elements) and bagua (the eight diagrams) to interpret nature, and usually resulted in giving people the most suitable and most beautiful places for living, with the advantages of good water supply, sunlight, a breeze in summer, protection from the cold in winter and good defensility.

The locating, for example, of towns and villages along rivers was for one side to face the water and the other a hill, whereby the buildings were positioned on the inner bend, which was continually being extended by deposits of mud and sand, the outer one steadily being eaten away by the force of the river's flow. "Ruiwei" is the name given to such topology, and such a sitting was considered by the geomancer as suitable for building on. The practice of employing geomancy to properly site towns and villages was deeply rooted in Chinese culture. An illustration is to be found in the following quotation from the book *Yangzhaishishu (Ten Books on Dwellings)*: "If there is a river flowing like a belt, high officials will emanate from such a place; generations of the same family will be intellectuals and bring honor to the family."

The deep-rooted belief that 'correct' siting can influence a place's fortune is exemplified by the village of Cangpo in the county of Yongjia, Zhejiang Province. In the 5th year of the reign of Xiaozong of the Song Dynasty (1178), a discussion was held with Li Shiri, the Guoshi (the reader of the emperor) to ascertain where best the village could be sited and what form its layout should take. An analysis was drawn up based on the theory of yinyang and wuxing, and the conclusion drawn that the village on the proposed site was in danger of being ravished by fire on the following grounds: according to bagua, gen and xin of the west are associated with jin (metal), but here to the west was Bijia Hill, flame-like in shape, thus foreboding fire; ren and gui of the north are associated with water with its fire-extinguishing powers, but here, where the village was to be sited, no pond existed to the north; jia and yi of the east are associated with wood, implying the risk of fire; bing and ding of the south are associated with fire itself, thus enhancing the danger of fire. Measures to combat the likelihood of fire were thus taken: a square pool was dug out to the south of the village; a long rectangular one dug out to the east as a barrier against the outbreak of fire in the wood and channels were dug around the settlement so that water from a brook could be channelled in such a way that there would have the water from the north. Now that the danger of fire was eliminated, the villages set about ensuring that the village was laid out in such a way that it would favor the development of literature. The name of Bijia Hill (a stand for the calligrapher's brushes) was utilized to create "the Four Treasures of the Study." The centre of the village was to directly face Bijia Hill, and a perfectly straight street was laid out to symbolize the calligrapher's brush. A strip of large boulder was laid on one side of the middle section of the street to symbolize the ink stick and south of the village a pool was dug to symbolize the ink slab. In addition the village was laid out on a plot of land square in shape, symbolizing the "paper". The "Four Treasures of the Study" were thus created. Finally, the whole layout was made to constitute a "big text" by having the streets criss-cross and grouping the beautifully shaped vernacular dwellings. It was the firm belief of the villagers that thereby the emergence of men-of-letters would be favored, generation after generation.

2. Configuration of the Streets

Roads serve to divide up towns or villages so as to form certain configurations. Major roads laid out as straight as the terrain allows, the aim being, however, to have the arrangement resembling as much a checkerboard as possible. If the division of the area into perfectly square blocks proves impossible for topographical or other reasons, some minor street will assume a zigzag or curved form. Such a street had the advantage of allowing the urban scenery to unfold gradually and not be taken in at one glance.

The way the old streets in Chinese towns and villages are laid out has a humane quality and reflects a way of life that has been led for centuries. People can walk at ease, enjoying the view of the different buildings and occasionally stopping to peruse the wares offered by the shops living both sides of the street. In the old towns of Northern China, many alleys are less than one meter wide and bear the picturesque names of yirenxiang (one-man alley) or yixiantian (a gap to the shy). Ordinary street, too are comparatively narrow, bamboo poles extending across the street from one building to another for hanging out clothes to dry. Commercial streets are busy, with the wooden houses compact and the tiled roofs in close array. Most shops have the sales area itself at the front and

Zhuma Pavilion in Chengkan Village, Shexian County, Anhui

In a pastoral scene with verdant hill and clear water in the country, roadside pavilions and cooling pavilions are often found, which gives us a touch of emotion and cordiality. There is a shrine on one side of the roadside pavilion, or one of the sides of the pavilion is a solid wall with a god niche for worshipping, while the other three sides are open. The cooling pavilions are open on all four sides.

the workshop behind, with people living upstairs. Country fairs and temple festivals add an even livelier element to the daily bustle .

The network of rivers in Jiangnan (south of the Yangtze River) provides an important communication and transport system. Both sides of waterways are lined with long covered walkways that protect the pedestrians from the sun or rain. Along the minor waterways, each family has its small, often elegant dock, used as a landing stage or as a place where the womenfolk can wash rice or do the washing. People living on boats ply the river, selling vegetables and other goods.

Within villages or blocks in towns, alleys and lanes are usually irregular in shape, and many come to a dead end, and are thus quiet as through traffic is eliminated. The point at which some alleys meet the road is occasionally given door openings and flying rafters, sometimes as many as two or three in number, as well as the odd bridge gallery. These serve to mark the boundary between a private residential area and the street and help give those living in one of the small alleys a sense of security.

Tall and large edifices such as bell and drum towers as well as bridge galleries were traditionally used to give contour to a streetscape. Large temples would be built at Y-shaped junctions to provide a focal point, and in some villages and towns, streets would be given T- or Z- shaped junctions, which were again set off by particularly imposing buildings. Thus streets, although basically simple, serve to lend the urban space from dint of their curves and straight lines and the way they converge and diverge, rise and fall.

3. Wayside Pavilions and Squares

Dotted about the countryside, with its green hills, lush meadows, clear rivers and streams, are the wayside pavilions and kiosks that have developed from the long and short pavilions of ancient times. According to a passage from Volume Nine of *Baikongliutie*, long pavilions were built every ten li, short ones every five, and served as a place for farewell dinners. There are also roadside pavilions open on three sides, the fourth being walled and containing a niche for worshipping Guan Yu of the village god. Some are open on all four sides to let in cooling breezes. Most are equipped with so-called beauties' rails. It was just these wayside pavilions that were described in detail by men-of-letters in order to express just how much they missed their friends and relatives back home and longed to be back in their native country. The poem Yanglingqin by Wu Cheng'en expresses such sentiments: "Now middle-aged, I wonder at how

frequently I am in foreign parts, and looking back to my native place, so many long pavilions I have passed." A feature of nearly every town or township is the square, serving to control the traffic, as a venue for markets, as part of the entrance to a building or, filled with water, as a harbor for ships and boats and later as a venue for general festivities. Crossroads often take the form of squares with the dual purpose of controlling the flow of traffic and providing a place for people to congregate. In old towns, squares were rarely planned in advance, developing gradually as the town grew and the need arose. They are generally irregular in shape and of moderate size. The entrance to a town or township, or where busy fairs were held, were often marked by a stretch of water which served as a harbor and later as a venue for cultural events and festivities. The market square is a feature of many a town or township and is given various names depending on the province. For the sake of easy accessibility, it is often located at one of a bridge or at the entrance to a village. Built round the market square are tea rooms, restaurants, washing facilities and shops. Very different in atmosphere from the bustling market square is the quiet and serene square at the entrance, for instance, to a mansion, a temple or a large vernacular dwelling. This type of square serves as a parking lot for cars and sedans as well as a place for people to congregate. Squares therefore developed as the need arose, and often had archways, town gates and market buildings accompanying them so that no two squares look the same.

The Artistic Characteristics of Vernacular Dwellings
—— Rusticity Hiding Preeminence, Simplicity Containing Inspiration

The artistic value of vernacular dwellings is not achieved by form but by implication. Structures are often simple, but the buildings, based as they are on complete philosophies of scholarly thought, nevertheless appeal both to the intellect and to the emotions. They devote themselves to serving all the senses.

Traditional vernacular dwellings can be easily comprehended. They are at times exquisite but never over-elaborate, imposing but never pretentious. Emphasis is laid on rational structure without losing sight of style; their decoration aims at giving pleasure, but is never meaningless. A variety of elements are combined in masterly fashion to produce a rhythmic whole.

Vernacular dwellings and nature are closely interwoven through the use of natural materials and the incorporation of nature into the basic design. Houses are appropriately dimensioned - man's well-being a primary consideration - and people are indeed given a sense of neighborhood, security and a feeling of closeness to nature. The spatial design of the traditional dwelling also has its social aspects, the courtyard serving as a center of communication, fostering neighborliness.

Extant vernacular dwellings are mostly to be found in ancient and remote villages and towns, those in Southern Anhui or Shibanzhai (Village of Stone Slabs) in the province of Guizhou, offering particularly outstanding examples.

The style of vernacular dwellings is so deeply embedded in Chinese culture that it often serves as a source of inspiration for official architecture, such as palaces, official residences, temples and mausoleums, too.

Many of the vernacular dwellings in southern Anhui have completely retained their Ming Dynasty style with its solemnity and primitive simplicity. Tier upon tier of corbel gables provide a wonderful rhythmic effect and the mainly horizontal lines of the buildings lend them tranquillity.

It is difficult to find words that adequately describe the elegance of vernacular dwellings, and the atmosphere created. Mei Shenyu, a Song Dynasty poet wrote the following on the subject: "Architects foster it in their mind,

Stone Slab House in Guizhou

The most representative of vernacular dwellings in Guizhou is the stone slab house. Stone slab houses are distributed mainly in suburban counties to the west of Guiyang City and in several counties of Anshun Prefecture. The stone slab house has its wall laid with stone block and roof with stone slab. Viewed from outside it looks as if it is entirely made of stone, but the actual structure is wood, it is the wood structure that bears the load, rather than the wall.

visitors comprehend the implications, but neither can express it in words. However, a broad idea may be told." It is similar to the phenomenon of enjoying the beauty of a poem, but not being able to explain why in words.

Surrounded by verdant hills and sometimes dramatic mountain scenery, many vernacular dwellings are often almost hidden from view by lush trees. It is particularly in early summer when the orioles sweetly sing that the elegance and picturesque appeal of these dwellings are at their most apparent. An evocative description of such a dwelling is to be found in the poem Xicun (The west village) written by Lu You during the Song Dynasty. "My cottage is small but snug, green moss is stopped at the newly-made brushwood door."

Ideally, the beauty of vernacular dwellings is both natural and artistic. The following excerpt from a poem written during the Tang Dynasty by Meng Haoran perfectly describes the atmosphere of a simple thatched cottage in a small remote village, "My old friend prepared chicken and millet, and invited me to his house on the farm. Green trees closed up on the village and verdant hills lay beyond the city wall. Under the window are the vegetable plot and the threshing ground. We talked about mulberry trees and hemp plants with a wine cup in our hands. On the day of the Chongyang Festival I shall return to see the chrysanthemums." The upright rows of suspended house in western Hunan, arranged at intervals along the banks of the river, its waters in autumn cool and clear, are an example of a grander conception of the vernacular dwelling, although compared with official buildings, it is still much simpler and rustic. The reason why vernacular dwellings interest us so much is that they are less limited and restricted by the formalities and regulations stipulated by the feudal administrators. In contrast to the buildings subject to the regulations laid down by the Yamen (government departments) with their cold and rigid style, vernacular dwellings could develop freely, resulting in a variety of different styles. They also exerted greater influence on architecture in general. Vernacular dwellings were designed to harmonize with their surroundings, the aim being an

Suspended House in Fenghuang County, Hunan

In the mountain area, a part of a building has to be supported in suspension in order to be built at an ideal location, thus giving birth to the suspended house. It has been developed under the condition that land sites are insufficient for dwellings. On the one hand it embodies a smart arrangement of living demand with technical capability, on the other hand it reflects the wisdom of the people. The contrast between the solidity of the building and the void of the suspended part underside evokes the sense of its hollowness.

elegant whole. This was achieved in part by the use of local materials, producing the profound lyricism of an ink painted landscape, and very different from the effect created by palatial buildings, splendid as they were. Importance was attached too to the effect the composition and color of different materials would have. Dwellings in the yellow loess highlands are yellow, too; buildings in the mountainous region of Guizhou, with its bizarre-shaped stones scattered over wide areas, were given slab stone walls and set against mountain slopes. Absolutely vital was the skill of the craftsmen, who had a store of technical knowledge. Personal skills in working the various building materials ran in families and slowly evolved over the years. The know-how necessary to produce vernacular dwellings of such quality exerts still today a certain influence on architectural design and guidelines involved.

I. The Appropriate Employment of Space and Compactness, Emptiness and Denseness Complementing Each Other

Although of simple structure, vernacular dwellings are rich in implication. The relationship between areas filled in and those left free is one of the underlying principles of traditional Chinese painting and that is also applied in the layout of Chinese vernacular dwellings. A case in point is a small town in the south of Yangtze River where, from the vantage point of an arched stone bridge, one sees row upon row of roofs and white unadorned walls. Beauty is here achieved by contrast. "No wind is allowed to penetrate these dense places but horses can race in the sparse area." Compactness, however, in the wrong place may result in a feeling of impenetrability while space wrongly applied can lead to a lack of unity. The roofs of vernacular dwellings are usually made to rise and fall to avoid monotony and lend variety to the walls as well.

This connection between architecture and painting is exemplified by the appropriate employment of space and compactness in vernacular dwellings. Da Chongguang, at the beginning of the Qing Dynasty, wrote in Huaquan that "emptiness and denseness complement each other; parts of a picture left empty are also beautiful." Tang Yifen wrote in his Huaquanxilan: "People only acknowledge a painting when the paper has been full covered; when parts have been left empty, it is not a painting. The overall situation, however demands that parts be left unpainted. Emptiness and denseness complement each other." This concept is to be found in many aspects of vernacular dwellings. Empty walls are the

empty spaces in paintings; several windows set in a wall give it a denser look. The empty spaces, for example, in the landscape painting 'A Corner' by Ma Yuan of the Southern Song Dynasty are like the spaciousness in the layout of a building.

There are many variations on this theme and can result in buildings that are clear and plain in expression but full of meaning, or ones that are immeasurably profound and not easy to understand. The contrast between the effects gained by a constant change in rhythm and, the simple and natural features is what makes vernacular dwellings so satisfying.

II. A Solid External Appearance and a Tranquil Interior, Artistic Concepts Playing a Primary Role

The Chinese have a predilection for physical enclosure. Large walls were thus also common in vernacular dwellings, providing not only defensibility and security but also the desired tranquillity within the building. These solid walls enclosed the interior space, shutting it off from the bustle of the world outside.

Xie He who lived during the Southern Qi Dynasty suggested the "Six Methods" in the preface to *"Guhuapinlu" (List of Ancient Drawings Appraised)*. These not only became the theoretical basis for later dwellings in China but the guiding principles for a theory of art in general. Of these, one of the most important was that artistic concepts should play a primary role.

Artistic concepts are also latent in vernacular dwellings. Chinese architecture differs from that of classical Greece in that the latter comprises the organic combination of blocks, while the former puts the emphasis on smooth flowing lines embodying artistic concepts that are richly varied and full of associative implications.

The roofing of North Fujian vernacular dwellings still retains the characteristics of the building regulations laid down in the Song Dynasty: The ridge at both ends, curves upwards and the four corners of the roof turn up too. There is not a single straight line involved. In addition, two curved fire-sealing

Eaves Gallery in a Residence in Dali, Yunnan

The beauty of simplicity and naivete is an important characteristic of vernacular dwellings in China. The eaves gallery in the photo is simply decorated with an easy style. The space of its top part was meticulously designed to mark a special impression.

96

gables on both sides are bow-shaped. It is just such features that add charm to a building, giving it both elegance and artistic quality.

III. Simple and Elegant Techniques Employed to Communicate Between Interior and Exterior

"Partitioning" is a technique commonly employed in the spatial design of vernacular dwellings, for the subjective observer often placing the objective world outside at a distance, making it seem unattainable, fragmenting and enhancing individual aspects of the view.

Railings, hollowed-out carvings, windows framing the scenery produce distance and partition heightening the sense of anticipation. Chen Jianzhai, a poet during the Song Dynasty wrote, "Gloss is produced from the flowers and leaves separated by the curtain." The curtain here serves to produce a linear rhythm, which in turn enhances the brilliance of the flowers. The artistic effect of communication between interior and exterior is one of the artistic techniques used in ancient Chinese architecture.

Separation as well as communication can be achieved not only by a bamboo curtain but also by means of doors or windows, the latter serving to frame the scenery, which can thus be fragmented into a series of beautiful pictures.

In the case of many vernacular dwellings, indoor and outdoor spaces merge into each other. Detachable partition windows are utilized as a means of bringing outdoor scenery into the room. The latticework in windows can be intricate and have various patterns in addition to the square. It can make the light inside seem to sparkle when seen from outside, or have the same effect as a papercut.

The visual impression obtained may be enhanced in effect by manipulating both light and scenery. Latticework not only softens the indoor light but also intensifies the sense of separation.

The sense of space achieved by this separating and merging contrasts well with the solidness of the buildings. Large, spacious courtyards were divided up by means of perforated walls or parapets to prevent the view being seen at one glance. The play of light was another important element and here the poetic element of the moon often played a part. The ancient Chinese character for 'bright' consists on the left of a window and on the right of the character for the moon. Windows of a building bathed in moonlight glisten. In vernacular

dwellings one element in the design is counterbalanced by its opposite: 'partition' contrasted with 'communication' and 'penetration'.

It is the simple beauty of these dwellings each adapted to local conditions and not in the main bound by official regulations, that stands out above all. Rooms are generally of open-frame construction, without ceilings, and on lower floors, the structure of the grid boards is also often exposed. Outer walls are frequently of plain brick and eaves hardly ever painted, protected solely by a coating of tong oil.

IV. A Richness of Decoration, Beauty not Characterized by Convention

Although often simple, vernacular dwellings can manifest a richness of decoration that gives them great elegance. Typical features of large, luxurious residences are the heavy and finely carved beams and trusses, the intricately patterned railings, the carved bricks and finely engraved metals and the rich carvings and paintings. However, as vernacular dwellings were bound by certain regulations, colored painting and drawing, for instance, were not allowed, colors are kept plain, giving the buildings a calm appearance when seen from a distance. From a closeup too, however, the exquisite craftsmanship is wonderfully apparent. Brick and wood carvings are often combined, plain walls and decorated eaves set each other off to perfection. The decoration of vernacular dwellings can be elaborate but is never overdone.

Some vernacular dwellings are profusely decorated. The outside walls, the space from the architrave to the roof, the doors and windows are all elements that can be decoratively treated. The impression the buildings give, however, is one of simplicity. In his '*Yigai*' *(General Principles of Art)* Liu Xizai wrote that baiben (plain ben) occupies the uppermost line of the ben diagram, meaning that the supreme pattern is precisely the original form. Baiben means a reversion from magnificence to plainness. In undergoing such a development, architecture reaches its goal, namely the beauty of simplicity.

The vernacular dwellings of Qiaojiabu in the county of Qixian, Shanxi Province resemble a magnificent painting. Rich ornamentation and the sheer inventiveness shown in the different types of roofs, the flush-gable, the round ridged-, the pitched- and the flat roof, lend these buildings subdued refinement and a beauty that is unconventional.

V. The Poetic, Pictorial and Musical Essence of Vernacular Dwellings

The sound of babbling brooks greets the traveller on arrival at the small village on the shores of Lake Taihu. It is a world that appeals to all the senses, giving vernacular dwellings their charm.

There is, for instance, a musical element in the rhythmic variation of the blocks and the contrasting strength of surface ornament. There are the smooth and elegant andante movements and climaxes reached in varying succession. The orderly arrangement of vernacular dwellings, the combination of spaces, the configuration of courtyards, the interweaving and alternating, the placing of doors and windows can be likened to the rise and fall, the rhythm, the different themes and the lingering sound of music.

Poetry is used as the synonym of beauty, and vernacular dwellings are the very poetry of architecture, just as they have a strong pictorial element.

The architecture of vernacular dwellings demonstrates mastery of the art of space, the poetry of space, in that it uses the different buildings to create an interweaving and alternating effect. The result is not only the interpenetration of one space with another but the heightening or lessening of tempo. The creation of an extraordinarily rich artistic environment containing all the basic elements of music, poetry and painting is its great achievement.

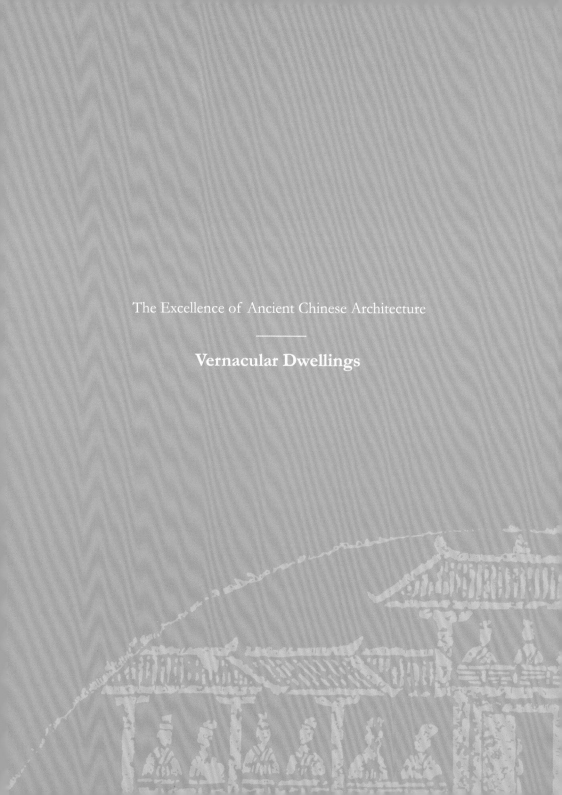

The Excellence of Ancient Chinese Architecture

Vernacular Dwellings

Notes on the Photographs

Earth Dwellings, Cave Dwellings and Siheyuan Compound

Ever since his existence on earth, man has concentrated his efforts on the provision of food, clothing, shelter and transportation. Stable dwellings, a prerequisite of the above, eventually developed into vernacular residential buildings. Various types of dwelling came into existence as a result of the ethnic variety and widely differing geographical conditions in a country as vast as China, and the building cultures represented by round storeyed buildings, cave-houses, siheyuan and other dwellings can be regarded as unique. The photographs in this volume illustrate, province by province, the vernacular dwelling characteristics of different areas in North, Central, South and West China, such as siheyuan, cave-houses, Zhejiang and Anhui dwellings, red brick, pile-supported and semi-pile-supported buildings and stone slab houses. These photographs do not only show beauty created jointly by Chinese artists and architects, but also manifest the spirit behind these Chinese vernacular dwellings.

Middle Gate of a Residence in Lishi Lane, Dongcheng District, Beijing

In siheyuan compound of Beijing, the middle gate is placed on the central axis and serves to separate the front courtyard from the inner one. As a major decorative feature, it is made extremely gorgeous and usually built in the chuihuamen, or floral-pendant gate style. The peripheral columns are not erected from the ground but hung on the beams passing through the central columns. Their lower ends are melon-shaped, and above them are exquisitely-carved petal designs and beadings. The gate roof is also very special, mostly taking the form of a double roof of continuous-span construction, generally comprising a plain-ridged overhanging gable roof and a round-ridged one, or, in some cases, two round-ridged roofs. The photo shows and example of the former type. The placement of a pair of stone lions was a rare practice limited to officials' mansions.

Arm-Corridors of a Residence in Lishi Lane, Dongcheng District, Beijing

Inside the pendant floral gate is a square inner courtyard, much larger than the front yard and constituting the core of the residence. On the northern side is the main building facing south, comprising an ancestral hall in the middle and, on each side, the living and bedrooms of the head of the family. The rooms in the east and west wings are where the younger generation live. At the ends of the main building side rooms and small yard are often to be found, and here is a kitchen, a toilet and storage space. Usually behind the main building are rear rooms for cooking, washing and accommodation for the girls. On the southern side, two verandas flank the pendant floral gate then turn northward, leading to the wing rooms. In some cases, arm-corridors stretch between rooms in the wings and the side rooms, extending to the main building. This photo shows the eastern arm-corridor in the inner court of a residence in Lishi Lane, Beijing as seen from the pendant floral gate.

Screen Wall and Pendant Floral Gate of the Cheng Family Residence in Wenchang Lane, Beijing

The siheyuan type of vernacular dwelling is very popular, and is represented by examples in Beijing. Such courtyards are square in plan. Their layout emphasizes scale, space and symmetry, with the central axis as the datum line for pairing the buildings on the flanks. The houses and yards are neat but varied, simple but graceful. A typical Beijing siheyuan generally has two or more courtyards. Entering the gate at the southeastern corner, one immediately catches sight of a screen wall standing opposite, the purpose of which is to secure privacy, while the gate's location at the southeastern corner is based on geomancy. Turning left, one will see a daozuo on the southern side and a pendant floral gate on the northern. The photo shows the screen wall and pendant floral gate of the Cheng family residence in Wenchang Lane, Beijing.

The Second Gate of Mei Lanfang's Home, Beijing

The home of Mei Lanfang was at 9, Huguosi Street, Xicheng District, Beijing City, where the famous actor at the Beijing opera and the first of the four great role players lived from 1950 until his death in 1961. The house faces south, and occupies an area of 716 m². A plaque with the words "Memorial Hall to Mei Lanfang" is now to be seen on the front gate. The photo depicts the second gate opposite a daozuo, which was built before Mei took up residence, and contains a large room formed by three central bays and one side one, previously used as a parlor. This gate is located to the northwest of the front gate and is the entrance to the main part, which is in sanheyuan style. Inside it is a small-sized screen wall.

Eastern Wing of Mei Lanfang's Home, Beijing

Behind the second gate of Mei Lanfang's home is a sanheyuan with a house to the north and wings to the east and west. The main room of the house took the form of a small parlor; the room on the west was Mei's study, and given the name of "Zhui Yu Xuan" (Literally "Jade Study"); and the eastern one, his living room. The study contains a large collection of plays, mostly classical editions or the only copies extant, and a landscape Zhang Daqian specially painted for Mei hangs on the wall. The western wing has been made into a library and over 30,000 valuable books pertaining to dramatic art, contributed by Mei's wife in 1965. A permanent exhibition of material relating to Mei's performances during cultural exchanges is presently located in the eastern wing, which is shown in the photo. Two small yards and a series of western rooms also form part of the residence.

Antecourt of the Kong Family Mansion, Qufu County, Shandong

The antecourt in this mansion is the most important of all the yards. It has a vertical rectangular plan, and contains on the northern side a grand hall, its main building, and two halls to the east and west respectively. From the grand hall a tile-paved passage extends southward, leading to a magnificent gate-shaped edifice called Chongguang Gate. The vast courtyard was planned for holding grand ceremonies. The Chongguang's Gate is a four-column, three-bay and three-storeyed chuihuamen with its four sides left open. It was originally calld Ceremonial Gate. The name of Chongguang derived from the Ming Emperor Shizong's inscription "En Ci Chong Guang" on the horizontal board hung on the gate. The gateway was kept closed except on occasions imperial edicts were received and great sacrificial ceremonies were held. The extraordinary depth of the courtyard and the noble cypresses lend the mansion a solemn and regal air.

Hallway of the Kong Family Mansion, Qufu County, Shandong

In the Kong family mansion, the main hall is linked with the second hall by an "T"-shaped hallway, a layout often to be found in administrative offices of the Song-Yuan period. There is no mention of this hallway in the records kept when the mansion was first built in the 10th year of Ming Emperor Hongwu's reign (AD 1377). The architectural form of the second hall indicates that it must have been added later, roughly when the Qing superseded the Ming Dynasty. It has a three-bay, six-frame and round-ridged roof in the middle and two double-pitch ones at the northern and southern ends, giving the appearance of a five-bay building. The central bay has doors on the western and eastern sides and side corridors in front of them. The beams are more slender than those of the second hall. They are made subquadrangular in cross section and painted using wood grain designs. When the door into the second hall is opened, and daylight from there allowed to penetrate, the mood of the hallway changes, and the onlooker is overwhelmed by the sheer radiance.

Northern Panel of the Screen Door of the Inner Court Gate in the Kong Family Mansion, Shandong

The inner court gate is located behind these grand halls of the Kong family mansion, and has the important function of sectioning off the inner from the outer areas. it is three bays wide and has a five-purlin roof, and is built in xuanshan style. Hung on the gate was an edict issued by the head of the family (titled Yan Sheng Gong) in his own handwriting, prohibiting any outsider from entering without permission. Implements for punishing violators, granted by the emperor, were placed on either side. There is a door between the central columns of the central bay, its northern panel has a mythical sheep painted on it as a warning to officials to remain just and honest when carrying out their duties.

Tower of Refuge in the Kong Family Mansion, Qufu County, Shandong
opposite page

East of the inner courtyard gate in the Kong family mansion, there stands a tall, four-storeyed brick tower, square in plan, and covered by a flush gable roof. At its foot is a square-shaped well over three meters deep. When danger arose, the well cover could be removed, making the tower inaccessible, hence the name "Tower of Refuge". Well built, and therefore ideal to defence, it is nevertheless refuge, rather difficult to date as it lacks chronological features. It was given the name "Dongkui Tower" in the Qing Emperor Daoguang's reign, and was probably built at a similar time to the Yiguantang Building. The photo shows the Tower as seen from the gate of the inner courtyard.

A Cave Dwelling in Zhangzhao Village, Sanmenxia City, Henan

The traditional Chinese architectural form is largely a curved-roof heavy timber structure roughly in a uniform style. In Shanxi, Shaanxi and other regions, however, where loess constitutes the main building material, cave dwellings took on various forms. The photo shows one in Zhangzhao Village, Sanmenxia City. Located on the margin of a loess plateau, it is built in sunken cave style, a highly unique architectural form. Subterranean buildings have many advantages. In addition to providing shelter in violent weather conditions, they offer accommodation that is cool in summer and warm in winter. This form of dwelling, too, offers better protection than other types of building in the case of fire, volcanic eruption and radioactive fallout.

A Residence in the Qiaojiabu Block, Qixian County, Shanxi

The Qiaojiabu Block is a complex of large-sized residences built in the late Qing period, each compound consisting of a primary court and subordinate ones. The former was the host's dwelling; the latter contained guest rooms, servants' quarters and kitchens, all lower and with flat roofs. The western and eastern wings of the former are single-pitch-roofed with the rain drained onto the patio. It is interesting that the single-pitch roofs of each pair of wing rooms in Qixian County are shaped like a ship side, contraflexure, representing a local feature different from both the traditional Chinese concave roof and the ordinary Western convex one. The photo shows the front gate of a compound in the block, leading to other groups of buildings through hallways and yards.

Courtyard No. 1 in the Qiaojiabu Block, Qixian County, Shanxi

Qixian County is located to the south of Taiyuan City and bore the name of Locus Qi in the Spring and Autumn period. For a long time the Qixian people mainly earned their living from trading. As early as the Daoguang and Xianfeng reigns of the Qing period, shops were a dominant feature in the county seat and its suburbs, and magnificent residences abounded. Among them, the Qiaojiabu block is one of the well-preserved building complexes, occupying an area of over 8,000 m^2 and consisting of 19 courtyards of various sizes attached to five residences and a garden on the northern side and three residences on the southern. The photo shows a view of Courtyard No.1 in the block, the many roofs are indication of just how numerous the courtyards are.

Interior Furnishings of the Qiaojiabu Block, Qixian County, Shanxi

The furniture of Chinese vernacular dwellings that has come down to us is principally of the Ming and Qing type. While artistically, Ming furniture is simple in form and has a free and elegant style, that of the Qing is of more elaborate craftsmanship. Perforating, mica-embellishing, tenoning, inlaying with mother-of-pearl on black lacquer are the favored techniques of decoration. The Qiaojiabu residences are strikingly furnished in Qing style, with the beds, small tables, cupboards and wardrobes displaying features typical of the north. The beds are large in size, providing places not only for sleep, but also for sitting cross-legged for having chats, receiving visitors, doing needlework, etc.

A Pendant Floral Gate in the Qiaojiabu Block, Qixian County, Shanxi
opposite page

Architecture reflects cultural ideology, proved here in the simple structure of a gate and door, reflecting national character, ethical principles, moral values as well as aesthetic interests, religious consciousness and level of education. The photo shows a pendant floral gate in the Qiaojiabu Block. The door itself is decorated with elaborate carvings. Above the lintel is a horizontal board bearing some inscription.

A Courtyard in the Qiaojiabu Block, Qixian County, Shanxi

Qiaojiabu is the most famous vernacular dwelling in Qixian County. It was originally called Zai Zhong or Middle-Holding hall because its owner went by the name of Qiao Zhiyong, meaning "Compromise". This block is not just a residence in the usual sense, but a castle-shaped building complex with all the characteristic features of Shanxi vernacular dwellings. Its surrounding walls are brick-built, solid, windowless, with an external height of a four to five-storeyed building, and thus ideal for defensive purposes. The houses themselves are mostly single-pitch-roofed; only in a few cases can gabled roofs be seen. The courtyards are largely rectangular in plan, pointing to the north and south, with the entrance placed at the southeastern corner. The photo shows a courtyard in the block.

Courtyard No. 2 in the Qiaojiabu Block, Qixian County, Shanxi

The compounds in the Qiaojiabu Block each consist of a primary courtyard as well as minor ones. The houses are single-storeyed except for the main buildings and those at the compound entrances that have two storeys. The photo shows the No. 2 courtyard with a reception hall, and an eastern and western wing. The hall entrance with fine carvings on the door is a clear indication of the building's importance. Accommodation is provided by houses in the wings. They mostly have two rooms; the outer for sitting, and the inner one for sleeping, with all doors and windows facing the yard. These suffice for light as the rooms are small in depth. The courtyards in Qiaojiabu are similar in layout, facilitating frequent contact between neighbors, a fact that reflects the intimacy of human relations in Chinese society.

Yixiantian Lane in Pingyao County, Shanxi
opposite page

Chinese traditional vernacular dwellings are mostly built of gray brick and provide simple yet comfortable accommodation in harmony with nature. The photo shows Yixiantian, or Linear Sky Lane in the old city of Pingyao. It is flanked by the high walls of the houses. The former is both neat and solid, massive and without windows, giving an illusion of stability and integrity. Such co-called "single-person passages" are very common in this old town. In complete contrast to the average urban street, they have a strong concealing effect, and serve as a link between the private sphere and the busy outside world.

A Residence in Shajia Alley, Pingyao County, Shanxi

Traditions, handed down from generation to generation in the evolutionary course of a national culture, reflect the uniformity of that culture and constitute one of the spiritual props of a nation. Chinese domestic architecture reflects the gravity and magnanimity, the optimism and the industriousness of the Chinese people. it demonstrates simplicity and craftsmanship as well as elegance and graciousness. Such qualities are to be seen in No. 34, Shajia Alley, a residence in the west district of the Pingyao County seat. The posts for tying up horses at the entrance bear traditional features. This simple but effective means of tethering horses shows great artistry and embodies the essence of Chinese tradition.

Entrance to a Residence at Shitoupo, Pingyao County, Shanxi

Traditional Chinese domestic architecture aims at creating integrated sights, it emphasizes the diversity of spatial sequences in building complexes rather than formal variety of individual structures. Chinese vernacular dwellings usually follow the same plan. An impression of great depth is achieved by the repeated development of secondary heights and delaying development on the principal axis. The photo shows the entrance to residence No. 3 at Shitoupo west of the Pingyao county seat. The simple chuihuamen and the courtyards behind it, visible from the entrance, demonstrates a natural gradation in the treatment of space.

A Cave Dwelling at Shitoupo, Pingyao County, Shanxi

Cave dwelling No. 2 at Shitoupo, west of Pingyao county seat, is a typical example of vernacular dwellings of the vaulted-room cave type. The construction of such brick-faced caves by better-off families was not for economic reasons, but because they were warm in winter and cool in summer, and their massive walls provided better protection in the case of fire or against theft. Although the buildings shown in the photo are weather-beaten, their original beauty is still visible. The fine latticework in the doors and windows and the elaborate cloud designs on the column capitals all demonstrate fine craftsmanship.

Decorations on the Eaves of the Zhu Family Residence in Xucun Village, Huoxian County, Shanxi / opposite page

Traditional Chinese domestic architecture was restricted in many aspects. For example, lacquer, color painting and dougong corbel bracket supporting were prohibited in the construction of vernacular dwellings. Nevertheless, some residences were exquisitely decorated. A standard model, the Zhu family residence in Xucun village, Huoxian County, is still to be seen. The four windows in its facade are decorated with patterns of various motifs but uniform and harmonious in composition. The decorated brackets bear elaborately carved woodwork imitating the inlaid and openworked designs on Shang period bronzes; and the color-painted patterns on the lintels are still faintly visible, and the rails over the first-floor eaves attract attention on account of the wonderful brick-carved peonies in full bloom, with their three-dimensional effect. The wood and brick carvings, as well as the solid walls and upturned eaves, all enhance each other.

Gate of a Residence in Pingyao County, Shanxi

The Chinese were great believers in the geomantic theory, maintaining that yin and yang were influenced by location, orientation and layout of a building, and if it were correctly sited, its owners' fortune would be favorably affected. Of particular importance were the appropriate location, orientation and size of the main gate because it was believed that this was where the elements entered. The photo shows the gate of a residence in Pingyao County. In front of it is a vast space; the courtyard on the other side tranquil. The gate, seen in general as a suitable structure for gathering the elements and absorbing the essence of the universe, is of moderate size and simply decorated.

Vernacular Dwellings in Pingyao County, Shanxi

The layout of vernacular dwellings in the Pingyao county seat shows great diversity. The photo is of the southeastern corner of the old city, the irregular roofs exactly reflecting the rhythmic arrangement of the houses. The contours of the roof rise and fall, resembling meandering lines occasionally broken. The outlines of the houses form numerous figures, similar in shape but of varying size. The vernacular dwellings in Pingyao can be both grand and plain, simple and complex; there is the straight and the curved; parts are left empty, others full of detail. Yet all is harmony, resulting in unique beauty.

Dangjia Village in Hancheng County, Shaanxi

The village of Dangjia is famous for its well-preserved ancient vernacular dwellings. Although the houses are regularly oriented, the streets and alleys vary in layout, forming spaces hidden among buildings; some winding abruptly and producing a dramatic effect. Many T-shaped intersections result in unex-pected and interesting sights. In the Shaanxi region, houses are arranged in quite dense groups and the resulting spaces between them seem to extend endlessly, lending impetus to the whole. Although the houses were for single families, they are closely linked, offering a sense of community while still providing privacy.

A Cave Dwelling in Xihou Village, Pinglu County, Shanxi

The village of Xihou in Pinglu County is famous for its cave-house compounds. The courtyards are commonly cuboid-shaped pointing north-south, so the south-facing caves have sun even in winter. The entrance is generally placed in the southeastern corner in accordance with the Eight Diagrams theory propounded in Wenwang's reign of the Zhou Dynasty. An average compound contains six cave-houses, of which one is on the northern side, serving both as an ancestral hall and a reception room. In some cases the northern cave can be increased to three, with the middle one as an ancestral hall and those on the sides providing accommodation for the older generation. Each compound is inhabited by approximately ten inhabitants. The floor is 10-11m below ground and 3-4m wide. As seen in the photo, the doors and windows are of similar construction to those of ordinary folk houses.

Interior of a Cave Dwelling in Xihou Village, Pinglu County, Shanxi

An ideal location is paramount in the case of cave dwellings. They then last some hundred years without undergoing serious damage, weathering better than brick structures. However, erosion caused by rain water can pose a serious threat. As soon, therefore, as crevices appear in walls and ceilings, these are immediately filled with earth. The photo shows the interior of a cave dwelling in Xihou Village. It is vaulted, and has a door and windows for light in front. The furnishings indicate that it must have been a kitchen. The whole gives a good impression of the simple life the local people led.

The Jiang Family Mansion at Liujiamao, Mizhi County, Shanxi
next page

Jiang Yaozu's manor in Liujiamao, lies in a deep valley in Mizhi County. It consists of a large and unique complex of cave dwellings. An eighteen-meter high fortified wall encloses the whole. The entrance comprises a vaulted gate on the southern side, behind which a winding cave-passage leads to a courtyard above ground. Here a steep flight of steps ascends to the first tier of a three-tier compound on a hillock, i.e. to the butler's yard. Climbing through a second cave-passage, one reaches the second and third yards, which are shown in the photo.

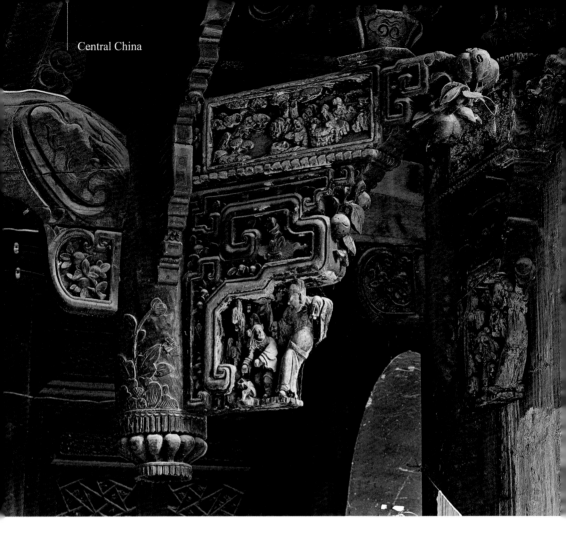

Wood-Carved Ornaments on the Chenggong Flat Brackets and Hanging Pillars in the Fuyuan Hall, Dongyang County, Zhejiang

In the Jiangsu-Zhejiang vernacular dwellings, the projecting eaves and other overhangs are generally supported by cantilever beams or chenggong flat brackets except for a few large mansions with dougong corbel brackets. The chenggong can be cirrus-shaped, take the form of pieces of bamboo, entwined vines, glossy ganodermas and other natural objects. The cantilever beams are also decorated with carvings to lessen their formal rigidity. During the early Qing period when architecture and sculpture in Dongyang reached their height, artisans devoted all their energy to the carving of decorated brackets and projecting eaves, handing down their skills from generation to generation, thus perfecting the technique. The chenggong and hanging pillars in the Fuyuan Hall are, with their exquisite carvings and vivid human figures and floral designs, perfect examples of the art.

Front Gallery of the Main Building in the Fuyuan Hall, Dongyang County, Zhejiang

The vernacular dwellings in Jiangsu and Zhejiang are commonly equipped with galleries under the eaves, which take the form of hall, full or winding veranda. These are to be found not only on the first floor but also on the upper storeys. The interior of the house is of open-frame construction with no ceiling, and even the top timber structure of the first floor in storeyed buildings is left open and merely adorned with moldings. In contrast, the space taken up by the galleries under the eaves is elaborately planned making a strong artistic statement. The photo shows a front gallery with crescent-shaped beams, decorated small beams and brackets, the carved designs of which stand out against the plain rafters of the eaves and the brick sheathing. The arched rafters atop the eaves gallery are additional members. They form a boat-roof-shaped top and lend the long narrow space remarkable artistic charm.

A Bird's-Eye View of the Fuyuan Hall in Dongyang County, Zhejiang

Many large-sized complexes of vernacular dwellings in Dongyang County still exist. Of these the famous residences include the Lu family mansion in the suburbs, and the Wuben and Fuyuan halls in the town of Baitan. With the passage of time, however, and the reconstruction that has gone on in recent times, these building complexes have lost much. The photo shows the Fuyuan Hall still in fairly good condition. The houses have massive gables coated in white, and their roofs suggest that the whole compound is laid out on a central axis. The plentiful carvings, the wooden members in natural colors and the whitewashed walls lend the buildings a plain and elegant effect.

A Corbie Gable of a Residence in Xidi Village, Yixian County, Anhui / opposite page

Xidi Village lies 5 km east of the Yixian County seat and extends 700 m from west to east and 300 m from north to south. Here, the vernacular dwellings lie in dense clusters but their layout is neat. They have many features that are typical of southern Anhui architecture, with its plain, refined and graceful style. The variety of roofs and gables, the contrast of gray tiles with white walls, and the decoration on the open balconies and closed gates are attractive to the eye; the whole in perfect harmony with the surroundings. The photo shows a corbie gable of a residence in Xidi Village. The massive wall with its series of steps constitutes an effective fireproof system, and its whitewashed surface is set off by the black tiles, imparting a pleasant and tranquil atmosphere.

Vernacular Dwelling in Xidi Village, Yixian County, Anhui

Solid external features and an inner tranquillity are typical attributes of Chinese domestic architecture. Large and solidly built walls are used both for functional purpose and their simplicity of form. Enclosed by such walls, residences are sheltered from the bustle of the outside world. Prevailing within is a calm and peaceful atmosphere while the impression gained from outside is one of rigidity. Depicted in the photo is a boudoir in Xidi village. The contrast between the solid white walls and the black tiled roofs produces a pleasing effect.

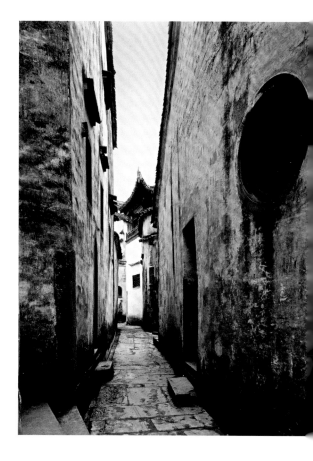

Vernacular Dwellings in Doushan Street, Shexian County, Anhui
opposite page

The walls of the vernacular dwellings of southern Anhui are generally coated with lime plaster and tooled with semi-cylindrical tiles which are arranged in butterfly pattern with the joints of concave tile rows covered by convex ones. The doors and windows are left in natural colors. The wall surface is largely white, occasionally dark gray, creating an atmosphere of calm. The buildings are mainly enclosed by level-topped high walls, with the exception of those sections that at the same time serve as house gables. These are stepped, and are higher than the roofs, adding variety and sophistication. The photo depicts the dwellings along Doushan Street in the county seat of Shexian. The roofs and gables along this long and narrow alley undulate rhythmically, and the general atmosphere has a simple local flavor.

A Moon Pool in Hongcun Village, Yixian County, Anhui

Moon pools laid out at the entrance of large-sized dwellings give the general layout an enclosed effect. This treatment was employed in many areas. Moon pools mirror the brightness of sunlight, display the clarity of water, and create a tranquil and pleasing atmosphere. The photo shows an example in Hongcun Village, Yixian County. The continuous stretch of buildings with their inverted reflections flickering in the water creates a dim, misty beauty-spot. The houses are mostly two-storeyed buildings, constructed side by side in neatly-arranged blocks. The elegant architectural form, harmonious composition and inverted images in the water combine to produce a sight full of simplicity and grace. The combination of buildings and water scenery is also characteristic of vernacular dwellings in southern Anhui.

Paifang Archways in Tangyue Village, Shexian, Anhui

Paifang archways in Tangyue village are the most famous group within this category of stone building in southern Anhui. At the entrance to the village, which lies 6 km west of the Shexian county seat, seven splendid paifang are neatly arranged and depict royalty, filial piety, chastity and righteousness in that order. Of them, five three-bay and four--pillar towering archways were constructed in Qing period, and the two three-bay, four-pillar and three-tier ones in the Ming period. They stand not in a straight line but along a winding road with a pavilion. Typical of the style of the Anhui stone-carving school is the bold and plain form.

Vernacular Dwellings in Wangkou Village, Wuyuan County, Jiangxi

The territory of present-day Wuyuan County was formerly under the jurisdiction of Huizhou district, so its vernacular dwellings, especially the corbie gables, are very similar in shape to those of southern Anhui. As shown in the photo, the structure of the outer walls of the residences is very simple, the exception being the gable tops, which are given detailed artistic treatment, and constitute a formal feature of Jiangxi vernacular dwellings. These step gables harmonize well with the double-pitch roofs, producing a variety of different scenes. Like many of the hamlets in this county, Wangkou lies at a bend in a small, idyllic river that winds its way through delightful rural scenery. A simple timber bridge is reflected in the water, creating an atmosphere of utter peace.

The Li Family Residence in Xinli Village, Longnan County, Jiangxi

The "Hakka" people in Suichuan County continued to build dwellings with traditional Chinese curved roofs, while in southern Jiangxi, the "fortified compound" became a popular architectural form. This type of dwelling resembles the earth storeyed building in Fujian, and is also referred to as an "earth-fortified compound." The photo shows the Li family residences at Shaba in Xinli Village, Liren Township, Longnan County. It is a fortified building complex, square in plan and four storeys high on all sides, including an underground floor. Each corner has a well-fortified five-storeyed watchtower, visible for miles around. Although in form fortified compounds slightly differ from Fujian earth storeyed buildings, in their layout and functional design they are identical with the latter, which suggests that the early settlers developed this type of building purely for self-defense.

A Residence in Suichuan County, Jiangxi

In Jiangxi Province, most of the vernacular dwellings have roofs screened from the outside with corbie gables, but in some areas of Suichuan County, Ji'an Prefecture, one can see the roofs revealed. The photo shows the Huang family residence in Caolin Township, Suichuan County. Here is a compact area of uniform houses, the so-called Caolin dwellings. Research has revealed that the inhabitants are mostly "Hakka" people, who migrated from the Central Plains to South China, but who have in general retained the distinctive feature of their original architecture, i.e. the gable-and-hipped roof, adopted in the Central Plains before the Tang period.

Interior of the Li Family Residence in Xinli Village, Longnan County, Jiangxi

The photo shows the interior of the Li family residence at Shaba in Xinli Village, Liren Township, Longnan County. It is identical with that of Fujian earth storeyed buildings. The timber structural members are exposed. Projecting balconies galleries are constructed from the second floor upwards. Auxiliary buildings such as kitchens, toilets and pigsties are located in the dim and quiet courtyard. Local records give no indication of when fortified compounds were first built, but the extant examples seem mostly to belong to the late Qing period. It is interesting that Jiangxi fortified compounds, Guangdong encircled houses and Fujian earth storeyed buildings are largely located at the same latitude. The correlation between the "Hakka" settlers and these three types of buildings is still unknown.

Rear Patio of the Zhang Family Residence in Liwu Village, Ganzhou City, Jiangxi
opposite page

One of the features of Chinese vernacular dwellings consists in an open inner space enclosed with a solid outer wall, which conceals life going on inside. The photo shows an interior view of the Zhang family residence in Liwu Village, Hubian Township, Ganzhou City. There is a large-sized room in the wing, the solid ceiling of which at the same time serves as the floor of a garret without clerestory windows. This attic can be reached via a stairway as seen in the photo and is used for storing grain and household wares. Below the stairs is a small storeroom for farming implements and other objects. The patio is paved with stones to protect it from being washed away by rain, and the deep overhanging eaves serve to protect the doors, windows and other wooden parts against the damp.

Vernacular Dwellings in Fenghuang County, Hunan

Chinese vernacular dwellings offer a wide variety of form; there are the seemingly impregnable earth-storeyed buildings and the compounds imbued with the spirit of the past; timber-framed or stone-built dwellings with a multitude of features. All these forms produce different aesthetic effect, they can manifest impregnability or a certain lightness, have an air of mystery about them or one of simplicity.

Lahaozhai Village in Fenghuang County, Hunan

Developed in different region, vernacular dwellings vary in both form and character. Diversity also exists in building material. Take the wall for example, there are those made of planks, those made of logs, those of bamboo or reed wattle and daub as well as others. The photo shows houses in the village of Lahaozhai in Fenghuang County, western Hunan. Their walls are built of irregular stone slabs, several centimeters thick, laid on flat. Thin stone slabs cover the roofs as well. The material used is simple and the style plain, creating an interesting effect. In southwest China, some blockhouses, several dozen meters in height, are also built of irregular stones, demonstrating the great skill of the local craftsmen.

Vernacular Dwellings of the Semi-Pile-Supported Type in the Seat of Fenghuang County, Hunan / opposite page

As man needs water to live, houses are often built along river banks, simultaneously facilitating communications. The walls of the buildings on the riverfront are supported by high timber, brick or stone piles to prevent the river causing damage. Such houses are even to be seen in Fenghuang County, a mountainous area in western Hunan. It is an intelligent way of saving space, too, employed particularly in situations where building lots are scarce. The riverside dwellings in the photo present an interesting example of pile-supported houses.

Partition Doors of the Pu Family Residence in Langzhong County, Sichuan

Viewing nature through windows, doors, yards railings, screens and garden structures has interested man since antiquity, the arrangement and decoration of doors and windows always have been given special attention. The photo shows a group of partition doors in the Pu family residence in Boxing Street in the county seat of Langzhong. The exquisite carving on the door leaves demonstrates an array of techniques and motifs. One marvels at the sheer mastery behind the carvings of exotic flowers and herbs, rare birds and animals, and scenes depicting musical instruments and the game of chess, calligraphy and paintings, symbols of happiness and wealth, longevity and good fortune.

Vernacular Dwellings in Mawangmiao Street, Langzhong County, Sichuan

The traditional form of vernacular dwellings frequently seen today goes back over two thousand years. Terracotta funeral models of houses from tombs suggest that the Han period dwellings generally had timber frames and xuanshan overhung gable end roofs or other types. Pictorial bricks from Chengdu, Sichuan, also provide evidence of the form of Han Dynasty houses, and show that beam-on-post and through-jointed frames were already used as heavy timber parts, just as they are today. The houses in the narrow alley shown in the photo are of the through-jointed frame type, and have black tiled xuanshan roofs. Their plain archaic style and unique tiled eaves lend the whole an air of times long past.

A Street in Langzhong County, Sichuan / next page

The enjoyment of scenery from a height was always a favorite pastime of the literati in China, and a bird's-eye view of a roofscape set off by whitewashed walls is indeed an attractive sight. This view taken from above, is of a street in the old city of Langzhong. The white walls, through-jointed frames, gable-and hip, and overhung gable-end roofs, are to be seen through the gaps among the black house tops. The projecting eaves provide shelter for pedestrians and peddlers. Its dense but well laid-out group of houses illustrates good integration of vernacular dwellings in the same quarters.

Vernacular Dwellings in Langzhong County, Sichuan

The placing of a taller building in a suitable spot so as to create a magnificent scene has always been a popular architectural technique. This includes the construction of bell-and-drum towers in villages and towns, archways and bridge galleries across streets, and large temples at Y-shaped forks in road. The photo shows the Huaguang Tower in the seat of Langzhong County. In this old city, the streets follow the lie of the land, with those sloping from north to south shorter than those running east-west. Maximum use was thus made of the more level plots while saving on precious building land.

Patio of a Residence in Langzhong County, Sichuan

Langzhong County is situated in a small basin surrounded by mountains. Typical of the Sichuan region, its vernacular dwellings are mostly of the through-jointed frame type and have a central patio and outer walls of bamboo wattle and daub. They differ from the houses of other areas in that they have widely projecting eaves mainly on account of the hot and rainy climate. These are supported by cantilever beams and generally serve as roofs for the pillarless verandas. The photo shows the patio of a dwelling in the Langzhong county seat. It is surrounded by four large-sized roofs and provides for ventilation, light and drainage on rainy days.

A Residence in Xujiawan, Ya'an County, Sichuan

Since early times, the Chinese have striven to achieve harmony with nature. The green of trees, the ripple of lakes and the glistering of brooks are natural phenomena that have long played an important role in Chinese culture. When constructing their houses, therefore, the Chinese often attempt to integrate such aspects into the concept as a whole. Depicted in the photo is a residence in Xujiawan. Nestling in a grove and surrounded by green mountains, it offers excellent living conditions, pleasantly cool, comfortable, tranquil and peaceful.

Vernacular Dwellings in Ya'an County, Sichuan

It is an example of the successful integration of vernacular dwellings into a pleasant natural landscape. The photo shows vernacular dwellings in Shangli Township, Ya'an County. The houses nestling in groves of shade-giving trees and surrounded by extensive fields form an idyllic scene. The houses are built in the through-jointed frame style frequently seen in Sichuan, and have black tile roofs with extensively projecting eaves.

Door-Gods on the Gate of a Residence in Yong'an County, Fujian

The custom of putting up icons of door-gods was one of the traditional ways of celebrating the New Year, manifesting not only one's respect for the gods and one's ancestors but one's desire to pray for happiness and exorcise evil spirits. Ancient texts recount that, during the life of the legendary Huang Di, there lived two brothers, Shen Tu and Yu Lei, who had the power to catch ghosts under peaches. As a result, people later made boards of peach-wood, carving them with icons of the brothers and their names, and putting them up at doors. This was later superseded by door-god iconography, which was no longer carved on wood but painted on paper. The door-gods of Zhong Kui, blessers, warriors and other mythical figures came into being. Depicted in the photo are the door-gods of blessers on the gate of a residence in Xihua Township, Yong'an County. The icons, with their exaggerated figures and bright colors, show people in pursuit of happiness. (Photo by Di Xianghua)

A Residence in Nan'an County, Fujian

Fujian domestic architecture is lofty in conception, profoundly philosophical, and boasts a variety of unique forms. In addition to earth storeyed buildings, there are many other unique types of vernacular dwellings, one of them being the Quanzhou type of folk house, i.e. the so-called red-brick culture, which also exerted an influence in Taiwan. The photo shows a residence in the village of Zhangli, near the town of Guanqiao in the county of Nan'an, Fujian. The village is a typical example of Quanzhou vernacular dwellings and was initially planned as a whole. As seen in the photo, the houses have outer walls with plain and varied designs in red brick. The roof-ridge ends are upturned to form dovetail ornaments, which add lively effect. This treatment was a customary decorative device in southern Fujian.

A Residence in Longyan County, Fujian

Fujian vernacular dwellings stand out on account of their large dimensions, variety of form and exquisite details, etc. The photo shows a residence in the village of Shanghang, Shanghang Township in Longyan County. The combined use of flush-gable, overhung-gable-end and hip-and-gable roofs gives the building variety. The gate is flush with the front wall, but its top is projected, and the side windows are decorated with vertical wooden bars or brick-carved openworked designs. The second floor has greatly protruding eaves, which serve as roofs for verandas that facilitate access. The effect produced by the white walls and black tiles of the roofs is completely different from that of the red-brick dwellings in Quanzhou.

Tianchenzhai Fortified Compound in Longyan County, Fujian / opposite page

Fujian earth storeyed buildings represent something very special among the Chinese vernacular dwellings. Gentle in appearance, they possess both a certain mystery and rigidity of spirit. There are detached and square buildings, the former grouped in compounds, with the houses varying in height and in the extent to which the eaves project, but well-arranged. They are, however, not easy to defend. The latter are well-fortified complexes with high walls on all four sides. Their regular superficies symbolize the dignity of the traditional patriarchal system. Nevertheless, the most striking is the round type of storeyed building. The photo shows Tianchengzhai, a four-storeyed oval earth building in Shizhong Township, Longyan County. Over the front gate is a projecting structure for defensive purposes. Originally, there were no windows in the outer wall from the second floor downwards, many having been inserted since for ventilation.

Interior of the Eryi Building in Hua'an County, Fujian

The Eryi Building, a representative of the colossal double-ringed storeyed buildings, is located in the village of Dadi in Xiandu Township. This building complex measures 73.4 m in diameter and has a 2.5 m thick earth wall on the first floor. It constitutes a multiple-unit building and has a ringed inner corridor. Remarkable is the secret gallery on the outer side of the fourth floor, onto which the rear door of all units lead for the purpose of gathering the armed forces in case of raids, and the fact that every unit has a zigzag sound-transmitting hole in the construction of the building for monitoring sounds from outside, but made impenetrable for enemy arrows. A network of tunnels runs underground, used as a drainage system in peacetime and as a way of escape in times of siege. Of all the earth-storeyed buildings, this is the most outstanding.

Huanji Building in Yongding County, Fujian

One of the most beautiful compounds among the Fujian earth storeyed buildings is the round Huanji Building in the village of Zhongnan, Hukeng Township, Yongding County. It has existed for over 280 years since its construction from the 44th (AD 1705) to the 48th year of Kangxi's reign. This is a three-circle building, the outer circle 44.68 m in diameter and four-storeyed, each floor containing 34 rooms and four common staircases. In the inner circle are ten parlors, each with a small patio, as well as two men's and two women's bathrooms on the inner and outer sides respectively. The photo is taken from within, showing the inner and outer circles of the building.

Main Gate of the Zhencheng Building in Yongding County, Fujian
opposite page

The Zhencheng Building is a round storeyed structure with a ringed inner corridor. It is located in the village of Hongkeng, Hukeng Township, Yongding County, and occupies an area of 5,000 m². There are a number of pillar couplets among its exquisite decorations. On the sides of the inner gate and in the ancestral hall are two couplets in a plain and fluent style beseeching the individual to work hard in order to achieve success. They are composed of two lines headed by the characters "zhen" and "cheng" respectively. The photo shows the main gate of the residence, its couplet also beginning with the two characters.

Interior of the Zhencheng Building in Yongding County, Fujian

Zhencheng Building is of the beam-on-post frame type and is constructed in two circles. The outer circle constitutes a four-storeyed building, each storey comprising 48 rooms. The whole structure is partitioned according to the Eight Diagrams division, i.e. by six rooms and one staircase for each floor. Between two "diagrams" is a fireproof brick wall with an arch door. The inner circle is a two-storeyed structure, the first floor containing parlors, and the second a ringed corridor serving as standing space for guests enjoying operatic performances on the stage at the center of the building. The photo shows the third and fourth floors of the outer circle, both with an inner gallery protected by so-called "beauties'rails". All four floors are neatly paved with plain tiles.

Huaiyuan Building in Nanjing County, Fujian / next page

The Huaiyuan Building is located in the township of Meilin in Nanjing County, in a mountainous border-area of southwestern Fujian. It is representative of the medium-sized circular earth storeyed buildings, and also one of the best-protected monuments as far as the interior and exterior structure of round earth dwellings is concerned. It measures 38 m in diameter, with four floors in its outer circle, each divided into 34 rooms and with four evenly-distributed staircases. In the patio at the center, an ancestral hall with an old-style private school stands facing the main gate. It has been given the literary name of "Sishi Study". Located within the one meter-wide winding corridor or the outer circle are pigsties and chicken coops, forming the second circle of the whole compound. The photo shows an external view of the Huaiyuan Building. In comparison with the nearby earth buildings, Huaiyuan has an air of dignity and a certain inscrutability about it, with its four watch-out platforms projecting from the top.

Shuzi Building in Pinghe County, Fujian

The Shuzi Building in the village of Yigujing, Pinghe County, is a three-storeyed round earth structure with a ringed inner corridor. It was built in the 54th year of the Qianlong reign (AD 1789) and is comparatively well-preserved. There is only one circle of dwellings, with the first floor projecting inwards. The whole building is divided into 26 units, each consisting of three rooms distributed on three floors and linked by inner staircases. Within the circle is a spacious courtyard paved with lines of pebbles radiating from the center. A call from here towards the building can echo. The photo shows a view of the building from the courtyard.

Tangwu Main Building of the Yu'an Residence in Meixian County, Guangdong

The "Hakka" people are the Hans who migrated southwards from the Yellow River valley in the late 4th (late Eastern Jin period) and early 12th (early Northern Song period) centuries. They are now mainly distributed in the provinces of Guangdong, Fujian and Taiwan. As a precaution against bandits, they generally lived in clans in remote mountain areas and undertook collective defence. Their dwellings evolved from single-family cottages, to multiple-family residences and finally to multi-storeyed buildings. Of these a unique type is encircled house, an example of which is the Yu'an Residence in the town of Nankou, Meixian County. It is divided into a front and a rear part. The photo shows the former, a roughly square complex consisting of a three-roomed main building and two wings. It is a large-sized building with a symmetric layout. The halls are not only magnificently built but also richly decorated.

Semicircular Building of the Yu'an Residence in Meixian County, Guangdong

The rear half of the Yu'an Residence is semicircular in plan and consists of a hall in the middle and 14 fan-shaped rooms on its sides. Between this part and the main building is a passage leading to the side doors of the whole encircled house. Built on a hillside beyond farmland, and laid out according to the topography of the land, the house is lower in front and higher to the rear. The semicircular building in the rear half corresponds to the pool of the same shape in front of the main building complex, thus making the residence into a complete round. Encircled houses constitute a unique architectural type in the "Hakka" region of Guangdong Province. They have a massive wall with small windows or are windowless. Such architecture promoted internal unity, mutual aid and external defense.

Roofed Bridge at Yanzhai, Sanjiang County, Guangxi

The areas where the Dong people live in compact communities are mountainous regions dominated by countless peaks, dense forests and small rivers. The Dong thus build their settlements in the main by rivers winding along at the foot of mountains, and so bridges represent important means of communication between villages. Dong hamlets are characterized by roofed bridges and drum towers, the former built across rivers near the villages, in style and color harmonizing with the vernacular dwellings. The photo shows an example at Yanzhai. It is a wooden structure supported by piers of long and narrow gray stone. The bridge has been left untreated, and impresses on account of its simplicity.

Vernacular Dwellings at Pingzhai, Sanjiang County, Guangxi

The joined timber storeyed buildings of the Dong in Sanjiang County were commonly built by relatives joining forces. Many houses of this type still stand in such villages. Construction thus proceeded along the following lines: several families of the same blood jointly cleared a building lot, employed carpenters to design and prepare beam-and-post members according to unified standards, and set up house frames aided by relatives and friends. Dong villages were generally built by a river, but stretches of water within or near the village were left for environmental reasons. Timber storeyed houses and their inverted reflections in water are an attractive sight. The photo shows vernacular dwellings at Pingzhai, Sanjiang County.

Vernacular Dwellings and a Drum Tower in Congjiang County, Guizhou
next page

The drum tower is another type of indispensable public building in Dong villages. The photo shows vernacular dwellings and a drum tower in the village of Gaozeng, Congjiang County. The dwellings are of the pile-supported type and mostly three-storeyed, with the first floor left empty and the roof built in the xuanshan overhung gable-end or xieshan gable-and-hipped style. The drum tower is a hexagonal structure looking like a multi-eaved Buddhist pagoda. The first floor is the highest storey, upon which desks of eaves in an odd number are superposed, gradually tapering off and ending in a conical roof. Rearing above the surrounding houses, drum towers not only constitute the center of Dong village, but are also an important landmark.

Decorated Bridge at Dipingzhai, Liping County, Guizhou

The roofed bridge was called gallery-bridge or storeyed bridge, and is also popularly known as decorated bridge. According to historical records, it originated around the early third century AD, but only in Dong village does it continue to be built as a customary architectural form. The construction of a gallery on the bridge floor aims at providing shelter from the wind and rain and protecting the wooden structure from weathering. It is also convenient for pedestrians who want to take a rest and enjoy the splendid riverside scenery from the extended bridge. The photo shows vernacular dwellings and a decorated bridge at Dipingzhai, Liping County. The pale tone of the hillside houses contrasts well with the brightly painted bridge, the whole presenting an air of utter bliss.

Vernacular Dwellings in Qianjiazhai, Leishan County, Guizhou / next page

In the mountainous regions of southern China, villages and towns are often built vertically, tier upon tier climbing up the hillsides to form a picturesque and elegant whole. The photo shows a panoramic view of Qianjiazhai, a Dong village of pile-supported houses in the district of Xijiang, Leishan County. Pile-supported dwellings have been built over a long period, and consist of small-sized storeyed buildings with a timber and bamboo structure, the upper floor for living, the lower for breeding livestock or storing household wares. The implicit beauty of Dong village manifests itself here in these Qianjiazhai dwellings, tier upon tier nestling in the forests covering the mountain slopes. They are also an example of the Dong people's capacity to adapt in general to the natural surroundings, the hillside site here being a case in point.

Qianjiazhai Village in Leishan County, Guizhou / preceding page

The layout of hillside dwellings clearly reflects the topographic features of mountain chains, this panoramic view of Qianjiazhai in Xijiang District of Leishan County being a clear demonstration of the point made. The village comprises pile-supported storeyed buildings with xuanshan or xieshan roofs constructed of tile or bark in a plain and unique style. Every house possesses a fireplace and the wisps of light smoke rising into the sky lend the whole village a quiet and pleasant atmosphere. An interesting feature is the line of bamboo tubes, referred to as " distribution of spring water through bamboo pipes ", running over a distance of several kilometers and supplying each dwelling with spring water. It functions all year round. The ceaseless flow of water and the constant stirring of the surrounding trees in the wind lend the scene life.

Superficies of a Bai Residence in Dali, Yunnan

Located between Mount Cangshan and Lake Erhai, the old city of Dali is famed for its scenic spots and the suburban dwellings distributed along the lakeshore. The photo shows a Bai residence consisting of three fang (the fang refers to a three-bay two-storeyed building) and a screen wall. This type of dwelling and the four-housed five-patioed compound are typical forms of the domestic architecture of Bai people. As seen in the photo, the screen wall is impressively located in the middle and the entrance, a roofed gate, at the southeastern corner. The screen wall has been given a three-sectioned roof and eaves with upturned corners. It is brightly decorated, the design being of great intricacy, and bears features typical of Bai vernacular dwellings. (Photo by courtesy of the General Office of the People's Pictorial)

Gate Construction of a Residence in Dali, Yunnan

In traditional domestic architecture, the main gate of a residence is generally positioned in the middle of a symmetric structure, but in some cases it is placed asymmetrically, generating a novel flexible effect. Bai people pay great attention to the construction of gates, and build two kinds: roofed and roofless. The former has a long history. It has a standard form that is richly decorated, consisting of a three-bay archway with high pointed wings raised on the flanks of the roof and magnificent dougong corbel brackets beneath the eaves. The latter was developed later, and treated in various ways, both from the point of view of form and decoration. The photo shows the main gate of a residence in Xizhou, Dali. It has no roof and boasts fine carvings, especially to be mentioned are those of a pair of animals, lovely in shape, exquisitely sculptured and realistic in style. The structure itself is free of the standard form.

Vernacular Dwellings in Sagya County, Tibet

Blockhouses constitute one of the principal types of Tibetan vernacular dwellings. They are built mainly of stone, timber, adobe and age earth. Some blockhouses have a height of eight or nine storeys, displaying the exceptional skill of Tibetan stonemasons, carpenters and earthmasons. Structurally, blockhouses combine stone or adobe walls with timber beams and posts, all load-bearing external and internal walls being constructed of block stone or adobe or a mixture of the two. The stone used is select, consisting of rather regular undressed block stones; the mortar is made of age earth, and no joint pointing is needed. The outer walls are made extremely solid by tapering at a ratio of 10:1. The vernacular dwellings in Sagya County are solely of the blockhouse type.

A Felt Yurt in Barkol County, Xinjiang

Ancient Chinese texts referred to the felt yurt as "vaulted dwellings" and "felt tent", while in Manchu language it is called "Mongolian yurt". This kind of dwelling has long been favored by the Mongolian, Kazak and other nomadic ethnic groups of China. The customs of the Kazaks are similar to those of the Mongols as their origins go back to the ancient Usuns, Turkis and Kidans and in later times to some of the Mongolian tribes. Their yurts are generally round. The skeleton is made of laths and comprises a network wall and an umbrella-shaped roof that is covered by felt sheets tied to the frame with ropes. In the center is a round patio. These dwellings are perfectly suited to nomadic life as they are easy to assemble and take down. The photo shows a Kazak yurt by the Haizi Salt Lake in Barkol County, Prefecture of Hami.

Interior of a Residence in Kashi, Xinjiang

As the Uighurs are Moslems, the interior furnishings of their houses is very much influenced by their belief, and the arcades, walls, niches, fireplaces, ribbed slabs and ceilings bear exquisitely carved decorations. Although ordinary dwellings are more simply adorned, colored paintings decorate the walls, and the elegant geometric design of the latticework at the windows is aesthetically pleasing. Here is an interior view of residence No. 158 in the district of Wusitangbuyi, Kashi. The furnishings are plain, but the arched covers of the wooden doors and their scroll designs have a beauty all of their own.

A Residence in Kashi, Xinjiang / opposite page

Kashi is mainly inhabited by Uighurs, and is called Kaxgar in their language. It lies in southwestern Xinjiang in the upper Kaxgar River valley, and is the center of southern Xinjiang. This old city has existed for some thousand years and was an important center of communication on the ancient Silk Road leading to Central Asia. In Kashi and Hetian, people live in compounds, the outer walls of brick or adobe and the houses with flat roofs of timber frame structure and compact-ribbed slabs. The layout of the housing is adapted to the terrain, and the whole bears typical characteristics of border towns in western China. Shortage of building land has resulted in two-, or more storey houses being built. In the photo is No. 49, Bageqi Alley in the district of Wusitangbuyi, Kashi.

Interior of a Residence in Yaduoqi Alley, Kashi, Xinjiang

Kashi vernacular dwellings are generally laid out around a courtyard, with single-storey houses interspersed among storeyed ones, and a peristyle placed in front, resulting in buildings varied in height and flexible in form. As the climate is hot and dry, no or few windows are set in the walls, and light is obtained through skylights, so the interior is kept relatively cool. How sparsely or richly furnished a dwelling is, and how much detail is involved depends on the owners' wealth. The photo shows the interior of a residence in Yaduoqi Alley in the district of Wusitangbuyi, Kashi. The large-sized tapestries and carpets, exquisite niches with carved scroll and floral designs, and the decorative borders on the walls all produce a splendid effect.

A Residence in Yaduoqi Alley, Kashi, Xinjiang / opposite page

The Uighur vernacular dwellings in Xijiang fall into four categories: Kashi storeyed buildings, Hetian a'iwang houses, Yining residences in western Asian style, and Turpan semi-subterraneans. The photo shows residence No. 6 in Yaduoqi Alley in the district of Wusitangbuyi, Kashi. It is a storeyed building. The influence of Islamic architecture is clearly to be seen as well as that of western Asia and the Middle East. The capitals of the peristyle vary greatly in shape and are elaborately carved. The intervals between columns and pendant pillars are decorated with pointed arches, above which are exquisitely carved and brightly painted floral designs, manifesting well the high artistic level of Xinjiang domestic architecture.

A Residence in Yining, Xinjiang

Yining previously fell under the jurisdiction of Ili. It is a beautiful city on the river Ili in western Xinjiang. As a result of being occupied for a time by Tsarist Russia, various types of buildings are to be seen, including houses in Central Plain style constructed by Qing Dynasty garrisons, residences in Russian style built by Russian noblemen during the occupation, and, of course, local Uighur dwellings in Islamic style. The photo shows Mijiti's residence in Yining. The gate and house have flat roofs characteristic of traditional Uighur domestic architecture. Decoration is chiefly applied below the eaves. The doors and windows are lacquer-painted in bright colors, producing a novel effect. Beauty here is achieved through simplicity and skillful workmanship, and the house glows with a vivid brightness against the azure sky.

Glossary

bay
a part of a building marked off by columns or pillars.

beauties' rail
also called "Wu State King rail" or "gooseneck rail." It is formed by a series of gooseneck-shaped bars and serves as the backrest of a long seat set between two columns.

black-head gate
a gate with two pillars supporting a lintel and double door leaves fitted within the frame. In the Song period, semi-cylindrical black tiles were laid on the pillar heads, hence the name.

brick sheathing
a layer of thin bricks spread over rafters to support the roof tiles, providing the underside of the roof with a neat finish and giving a modicum of protecting against dust and draughts.

bridge gallery
a covered flyover joining the second or third storeys of two buildings on different sides of a street.

central bay
section between the central columns in the facade of a building.

chiwen or chiwei
ridge-end ornaments in the shape of an animal's head; used in ancient Chinese architecture to decorate the ends of the main ridge of a house.

chuihuamen of floral-pendant gate
the second gate of an old-style residence. It has a vaulted top with carved and painted ornaments.

coffered ceiling
a ceiling covered with finely carved sunken panels.

compact-ribbed slab
a structural member made of horizontal- and vertical-ribbed slabs. It serves to partition space or fulfill a load-bearing function as beams and posts.

corbie gable
a gable with a series of steps, or steplike projections, rising towards the ridge-pole of a building, exceeding the roof in height, and with prominent moldings and tile-covered ridges.

crescent-shaped beam
slightly arched top-beam in the beam frame of a round-ridged roof.

cross ridge
a roof ridge formed by two horizontal ridges intersecting as a cross in plan.

daozuo
a building lying on the principal axis of a residence and opposite the main building, i.e. usually facing north.

depth
distance between the front and back peripheral columns.

door opening
leafless door in the wall of an enclosure, corridor, pavilion, etc.

double or multiple eaves
eaves of a roof in two or more tiers.

double-pitch roof
gabled roof.

efang, or architrave
tie-beam between two peripheral columns. It may support one or more intermediate bracket sets in buildings with dougong.

eaves tile, or tile end
end of a semi-cylindrical tile at the eaves. It is semicircular (in early times) or circular (from the Qin-Han period onward) and often has an inscription or a design.

facing tile
tile for surfacing walls of mud or other material.

finishing coat
decorative surface of a structural member (column, beam, wall, floor, etc.)

fireplace
a hollow made in a floor to hold an open fire for cooking food, heating water and drying clothes.

fire-sealing gable
i.e. corbie gable. It can prevent otherwise disastrous fires from spreading to neighboring buildings, hence the name.

flat roof
toof with a drainage pitch less than 10%.

flat tile
roof tile with the cross section having a curvature of less than a semicircle.

gable
wall at either end of a building.

gate construction
the general designation of the parts of a residence gate in traditional Chinese architecture, including overhang eaves, drum-shaped stone blocks on both sides of the gate, ornaments above the door, steps, and side walls. Simple small-sized gate construction, however, only have the first.

hipped roof
a roof with four slopes, a horizontal ridge at the top and four hips or "sloping ridges" at the point where two adjacent slopes meet. In traditional Chinese architecture, the slopes are slightly curved and the corners of the roof upturned.

"horse-racing" buildings
storeyed buildings on the sides of a square, with a ringed veranda built along the inner sides.

inverted-V corbel bracket
a structural member placed on an efang lintel for load-bearing. It was used from the late Han to the Tang period.

jinjian
one of the end sections of a seven-bay building.

joist
also called longgu. One of the small beams or posts ranged parallel from wall to wall to support a floor, ceiling or partition.

juzhe, or raising-and depression
method of determining the pitch and curvation of a roof.

nipples
projections on the back of ancient facing tiles for better attachment.

ornamental perforated window
window with an openwork design usually composed of smoothened bricks or tiles.

open-frame construction
architectural style of leaving the rafters and brick sheathing open, dispensing with a ceiling and other coverings.

overhanging eaves
extending a roof beyond the outer wall or peripheral columns of a building.

paifang archway
a decorated entrance in the form of an arch erected in front of a group of buildings, at the access to a city's sector or at an important road junction.

pailou memorial arch
free-standing high gateway joined overhead by eaves supported by dougong corbel brackets.

parapet
low protective wall at the edge of a flat roof, a terrace or a city-wall.

partition
a vertical structural member dividing the interior space of a building.

partion board
interior or exterior wooden element for spatial division.

pavilion roof
conical, pyramidal or polygonal pinnacled roof.

perforated wall
an openworked wall serving to screen off, to provide shade or ventilation, and as decoration.

pitched roof
roof with a drainage pitch of more than 10%.

plain brick wall
an unwhitewashed and unfaced brick wall. The brick joints are filled with cement mortar which is, in some cases, then painted white. Such a wall has a neat and plain appearance.

platform
the base of a building raised above the ground for load-bearing and protection against damp.

plinth
round or square base made of stone to support a column.

projecting eaves
eaves below the roof of a double- or multi-eaved building.

purlin
one of the horizontal timbers supporting the rafters of a roof.

rafter
one of the timbers placed on and across the purlins, circular or square in cross section, and used for supporting a roof and its sheathing.

roofing
covering layers of a roof comprising a surface and a base, the former to keep out the rain, the latter for supporting the surface, pitching the roof and transferring the load.

round-ridged roof
roof with the joint between the front and back slopes made round in cross section.

rowlock wall
a hollow wall made of bricks on edge placed as headers and stretchers in Flemish bond.

sanheyuan
a compound with the houses built on three sides of a yard and a wall on the fourth.

screen wall
a screen-like wall built outside or inside a gate.

semi-cylindrical tile
semicircular-sectioned roof tile.

shallow-vaulted roof
a roughly flat roof slightly-raised in the middle to form a cambered surface for draining off the rain down the two slopes.

shaojian
one of the sections next to the subcentral bays of a five- or seven-bay building.

side room

one of the two small rooms at the ends of the main buikding.

siheyuan

traditional Chinese dwelling of the compound type with houses built on the four sides of a courtyard and usually without windows in the enclosing walls.

sill window

a type of window placed on a low wall in combination with lattice doors and to be found in palatial buildings and temples.

smoothened-brick wall

a wall built of tight-fitted bricks which are carefully ground to the required size beforehand.

subcentral bay

one of the two sections next to the central bay of a building.

tangwu

also called zhengfang. The main building on the principal axis of a residence.

through-jointed frame

a type of timber frame in ancient Chinese architecture. It has no beams and the pulins are directly supported by columns with joints passing. through column tops.

tianjing

1. Patio small space open to the sky and used in buildings or yards enclosed by houses on four sides or by those on three sides and a wall on the fourth.
2. Ceiling or caisson in an ancient building.

veranda

a roofed open gallery attached to the exterior of a building and often erected in gardens and courtyards. It served both to link up with, and separate from the space outside.

well pavilion

a pavilion built above a well, with the center of the top sometimes left open.

width

the distance between the two end columns in the facade of a building.

wing room

one of the buildings flanking a courtyard in front of the main building.

xieshan gable-and-hipped roof

a hipped roof with small gables at the two ends, i.e. a roof with its upper part gabled and its lower part hipped.

xieshan flush gable roof

two sloped roof, flush with the gables or slightly lower than them.

zhengfang

see tangwu.

Chronology of Major Events
in the History of Chinese Architecture

Christian era	Chinese Dynastic Years	Events or Achievements
The Neolithic Age		
ca. 4800 BC		Sites of ganlan buildings (pile-supported structures with wooden floor above the ground) of Hemudu Culture were unearthed in the northeast of Hemudu Village in Yuyao County, Zhejiang Province.
ca. 4500 BC		Sites of Various kinds of primitive houses of Yangshao Culture, including a big house square in plan were unearthed in Banpo Village near Xi'an, Shaanxi Province.
2310~2378 BC		A sacrificial altar of Liangzhu Culture was unearthed at Yaoshan in Yuhang County, Zhejiang Province.
ca. 3000 BC		Temple of Goddess of Hongshan Culture was discovered at Niuheliang in Lingyuan County, Liaoning Province.
The Shang Dynasty		
1900~1500 BC		An Early Shang site of a high-terrace palatial complex was unearthed at Erlitou Village in Yanshi County, Henan Province.
17th~11th c. BC		Rectangular houses with rammed earth foundations and walls were unearthed in present Zhengzhou, Henan Province.
1384 BC	15th year, Pangeng	Capital of the Shang was moved to Yin where the Late Shang capital was constructed, which was unearthed and referred to as the Yin Ruins at Xiaotun Village in Anyang, Henan Province.
The Western Zhou Dynasty		
1095 BC	10th year, Chengwang	An ancestral temple of the Zhou Court was unearthed at Fengchu Village in Qishan County, Shaanxi Province.
The Spring and Autumn Period		
475 BC	45th year, Jingwang	Rules for capital planning of the Zhou Court were recorded in the Survey on Construction Work collected in the Ritual of Zhou, in which it was regulated that the Ancestral Temple was to be located to the left of the palace, and the Altar of Land and Grain, to its right.
The Warring States Period		
350~207 BC		Site of Xianyang Palace of the Qin State, a high-terrace building complex, was unearthed at Xianyang, Shaanxi Province.
The Qin Dynasty		
221 BC	26th year, Shi Huang Di	The Qin conquered the six states and built palaces in styles to imitate those of the conquered states on the northern sloping fields of Xianyang. An army of 300,000 men, led by Meng Tian, was sent to drive out the northern nomadic Hun invasions and to build the Great Wall from Lintao (in present-day Gansu province) in the west to Liaodong (the east of present-day Liaoning Province) in the east. Capital Xianyang was constructed and extended.
221~210 BC	26th~37th years, Shi Huang Di	Construction of Shi Huang Di's mausoleum started in Lintong, Shaanxi Province.
212 BC	35th year, Shi Huang Di	Construction of the Epang (or Efanggong) Palace began on the south bank of the Wei River, Xianyang.
The Western Han Dynasty		
200 BC	7th year, Gaozu	Palatial city in Chang'an (present-day Xi'an) was under construction and Changle Palace (Palace of Everlasting Happiness) was erected.
199 BC	8th year, Gaozu	Construction of Wei Yang palace started. The Palace was completed in the next year.
140~87 BC	Reign period of Wudi	Construction of Maoling Tomb (the Mausoleum of Emperor Wudi) started in Xingping County, Shaanxi Province.
138 BC	4th year, Jianyuan, Wudi	Shang Lin Garden of the Qin was extended in a vast area of 300 li across with 70 detached palaces included.
127 BC	2nd year, Yuanshuo, Wudi	The Great Wall with watchtowers, passes and beacon towers was reconstructed. Later on, the Great wall underwent five large-scale reconstruction works.

Christian era	Chinese Dynastic Years	Events or Achievements
104 BC	1st year, Taichu, Wudi	Jian Zhang Palace was built in the western outskirts of Chang'an City.
101 BC	4th year, Taichu, Wudi	Ming Guang Palace was built in the City of Chang'an.
32 BC	1st year, Jianshi, Chengdi	Altars for offering sacrifices to God of Heaven and God of Earth were erected in the southern and northern suburbs of Chang'an respectively. Thereafter the locations of the Altar of Heaven and the Altar of Earth in the planning of the capital city were so established as a rule.
4 AD	4th year, Yuanshi, Pingdi	Mingtang, Biyong (halls for handling state affairs and promulgating politics as well as schooling) and Lingtai (Terrace of Spirit) were erected inside and outside Chang'an.
The Xin Dynasty		
20 AD	1st year, Dihuang, Wang Mang	More than ten palaces, including Jian Zhang Palace, were demolished. The disassembled materials were used to build eleven buildings in the southern suburbs of Chang'an, known as the Nine Temples of Wang Mang historically.
The Eastern Han Dynasty		
68 AD	11th year, Yongping, Mingdi	Baima Si (the Temple of White Horse) was erected in Luoyang.
Period of the Three Kingdoms		
220 AD	1st year, Huangchu, Wendi of the Wei	Cao Pi founded the Kingdom of Wei with its capital moved from Yecheng to Luoyang.
221 AD	1st year, Zhangwu, the Shu Han	Liu Bei founded the Kingdom of Shu Han, making Chengdu (in present-day Sichuan province) its capital.
229 AD	8th year, Huangwu, the Wu	Sun Quan moved the capital of the Kingdom of Wu from Wuchang to Jianye (present-day Nanjing). The capital city with the palace were then constructed.
235 AD	3rd year, Qinglong, Mingdi of the Wei	The Palace of Luoyang of the Wei Court was built at Luoyang.
237 AD	1st year, Jingchu, Mingdi of the Wei	The Garden of Fragrant Forest (Fang Lin Yuan) was completed and the Hill of Jingyang was piled up in Luoyang
The Jin Dynasty		
ca. 300 AD	ca. 1st year, Yongkang, Huidi	Shi Chong built a garden at the Golden Ravine in the northeastern outskirts of Luoyang, known as the Garden of Golden Ravine.
332 AD	7th year, Xianhe, Chengdi	The Palace of Jiankang was built in Jiankang (present-day Nanjing).
347 AD	3rd year, Yonghe, Mudi	An imperial garden called Hualin Garden was built at the southern bank of Xuanwu Lake in Jiankang. About a hundred years later, the Song of the Southern Dynasties built another garden called the Pleasure Garden to the east of Hualin Garden.
353~366 AD		Mogao Grottoes at Dunhuang, in present-day Gansu Province, were first dug out.
400 AD	4th year, Long'an, Andi	Buddhist Monk Huichi built the Temple of Samantabhadra (present-day the Wannian Temple) at Mount Emei in Sichuan.
413 AD	9th year, Yixi, Andi	Helianbobo built Tongwancheng, capital city of the Great Xia Dynasty (in presentday Inner Mongolia).
The Northern and Southern Dynasties		
452~464 AD	Wenchengdi, Northern Wei	Yungang Grottoes at Datong, Shanxi, were first hollowed out.
494~495 AD	18th~19th years, Taihe, Northern Wei	Longmen Grottoes at Luoyang, Henan, were first hollowed out.
513 AD	2nd year, Yanchang, Northern Wei	Grottoes of Bingling Temple, a Buddhist cave temple in Gansu, was built.
516 AD	1st year, Xiping, Northern Wei	Wooden Pagoda of the Temple of Everlasting Tranquillity (Yongning Temple) was erected up in Luoyang.
523 AD	4th year, Zhengguang, Northern Wei	Brick Pagoda of the Songyue Temple at Dengfeng in Henan was built.
The Sui Dynasty		
582	2nd year, Kaihuang, Wendi	Yuwen Kai was appointed to design and construct the capital city Daxing (present-day Xi'an), which was renamed as Chang'an in the Tang Dynasty.
586	6th year, Kaihuang, Wendi	Construction of the Longzang Buddhist Temple at Zhengding, Hebei, started. The temple was renamed as the Longxing Temple in the reign period of Emperor Kangxi of the Qing Dynasty.
595	15th year, Kaihuang, Wendi	Palace of Benevolence and Longevity (Ren Shou Gong) was built in Daxing, capital of the Sui Dynasty.
607	3rd year, Daye, Yangdi	One million men were sent to repair and restore the Great Wall.
611	7th year, Daye, Yangdi	The Four-Gate Pagoda, a single-storeyed pagoda, of Shentong Temple in Licheng, Shandong, was built.

Christian era	Chinese Dynastic Years	Events or Achievements
The Tang Dynasty		
618~916		Double-storeyed single-sealed dwelling houses came into being, while multi-storeyed buildings became on the wane.
627~648	Period of Zhenguan, Taizong	Mount Hua in Shaanxi, one of the Five Sacred Mountains in ancient China, was granted as the Golden Heavenly King, where the Temple of Western Sacred Mountain was built.
630	4th year, Zhenguan, Taizong	Orders were given to erect Confucian Temples in the schools of prefectures and counties all over the country.
636	10th year, Zhenguan, Taizong	Construction of Zhaoling Tomb (the Mausoleum of Emperor Taizong) began in Liquan County, Shaanxi.
651	2nd year, Yonghui,Gaozong	Taziks (the Arabian Empire) sent envoys to the Tang Court. Since then, the Islamic architecture came into being in China.
7th century		Huaisheng Si (literally, the Mosque in Memory of the Saint) was first built in Guangzhou, Guangdong.
652	3rd year, Yonghui,Gaozong	The Great Wild Goose Pagoda of Ci'en Temple in Chang'an (present-day Xi'an) was built.
669	2nd year, Zongzhang,	The Pagoda of Xuanzang was built in Xingjiao Temple in Chang'an.
681	1st year, Kaiyao, Gaozong	The Pagoda of Xiangji Temple in Chang'an was built.
683	1st year, Hongdao, Gaozong	Construction of Qianling Tomb (the Mausoleum of Emperor Gaozong) began in Qianxian County, Shaanxi.
707~709	1st~3rd years, Jinglong,Zhongzong	The Small Wild Goose Pagoda of Jianfu Temple in Chang'an was built.
714	2nd year, Kaiyuan,Xuanzong	Construction of Xingqing Palace in Chang'an started.
722	10th year, Kaiyuan, Xuanzong	The Tianchang Taoist Temple in Youzhou (present-day Beijing) was first built. The Temple was renamed as Baiyun Guan, or the Temple of White Clouds, in the early Ming Dynasty.
724	12th year, Kaiyuan, Xuanzong	Jianfu Palace at the foot of Qingcheng Mountain in Sichuan was first built.
725	13th year, Kaiyuan, Xuanzong	The Huaqing Pool with a detached palace was built at Lishan in Lintong County, Shaanxi. The Qujiang Pool with a recreation garden was built in Chang'an.
782	3rd year, Jianzhong, Dezong	The Main Hall of Nanchan Temple in Mount Wutai, Shanxi, was built.
857	11th year, Dazhong, Xuanzong	The Eastern Hall of Foguang Temple in Mount Wutai, Shanxi, was built.
The Five Dynasties		
956	3rd year, Xiande,Shizong, Late Zhou	The Later Zhou made Kaifeng the capital, and then, extended it on the basis of the capital of the Later Liang and Later Jin. Thereafter, Kaifeng was further developed especially when it was made capital of the Northern Song Dynasty.
959	6th year, Xiande,Shizong, Late Zhou	The Pagoda of Yunyan Temple at Suzhou, Jiangsu, was built.
The Northern Song and Liao (Khitan)Dynasties		
960~1279		Style and form of local dwelling houses were gradually finalized with less difference from those of the Qing period.
964	2nd year, Qiande,Taizu, the Song	The Temple of Central Sacred Mountain at Songshan, Henan, was renovated.
971	4th year, Kaibao,Taizu, the Song	The Pavilion of Buddha Fragrance (Foxiang Ge) at Longxing Temple in Zhengding, Hebei, was first built with a 24-metre-high bronze statue of Guanyin (Goddess of Mercy, or Avalokitesvara) housed in.
977	2nd year, Taipingxingguo,Taizong, the Song	The Longhua Pagoda was erected in Shanghai.
984	2nd year, Tonghe,Shengzong, the Liao	The Guanyin Pavilion and the Entrance Hall of Dule Temple at Jixian County in present day Tianjin were built.
996	14th year, Tonghe,Shengzong, the Liao	Libai Si of Niujie, or the Mosque of Ox Street, in Beijing was first built.
1009	2nd year, Dazhongxiangfu,Zhenzong, the Song	Tiankuang Dian (literally, the Hall of Godsend) of Dai Miao (Temple of Eastern Sacred Mountain) was built on the foot of Mount Tai, Shandong. Temple of Princess Aurora was built on the top of Mount Tai.
1009	2nd year, Dazhongxiangfu,Zhenzong, the Song	The Ashab Mosque at Quanzhou, Fujian, was first built.

Christian era	Chinese Dynastic Years	Events or Achievements
1038	7th year, Chongxi,Xingzong, the Liao	The Bhagavat Storage Hall (Bojia Jiaozang Dian) of the Lower Huayan Temple in Datong, Shanxi, was built.
1052	4th year, Huangyou,Renzong, the Song	The Hall of Sakyamuni (Moni Dian) of Longxing Temple in Zhengding, Hebei, was built.
1056	2nd year, Qingning,Daozong, the Liao	The Pagoda of Sakyamuni, or the Wooden Pagoda, of Fogong Temple at Yingxian, Shanxi, was erected.
1100	3rd year, Yuanfu,Zhezong, the Song	Li Jie finalized the book Building Standard, or treatise On Architectural Methods, which was promulgated by the Song Court in 1103 as building codes for design and construction works.
1102	1st year, Chongning,Huizong, the Song	The Shengmu Hall, or the Hall of Sacred Mother, of Jin Ci, a memorial temple of Jin, in Taiyuan, Shanxi, was restored.
1115	5th year, Zhenghe,Huizong, the Song	It is recorded that there were more than ten thousand workers everyday forced to build Mingtang for the emperor in Kaifeng.
1125	7th year, Xuanhe,Huizong, the Song	The Chuzu Nunnery, or the Hall of Patriarch, of Shaolin Temple in Dengfeng, Henan, was built.
12th century		The Minaret of Light was built in Huaisheng Si, or the Mosque in Memory of the Saint, in Guangzhou, Guangdong.
The Southern Song and Jin (Jurchen)Dynasties		
12th century		Han Tuozhou built his personal garden, called the Southern Garden, in Lin'an (present-day Hangzhou). Han Shizong built his personal garden, called Meigang Garden (literally, the Garden of Plum Blossom Ridge), in Lin'an.
1138	8th year, Shaoxing,Gaozong, the Song	The Song Court moved to Lin'an where the temporary palace was arranged. Lin'an was then decided upon as the temporary capital and was extended.
1150	2nd year, Tiande,Qingdi, the Jin	Wanyan Liang, emperor of the Jurchen (Jin), renamed Youzhou (present-day Beijing) as the Middle Capital of the Jurchen, and assigned Zhang Hao and Kong Yanzhou to the construction of the Middle Capital.
1163	3rd year, Dading,Shizong, the Jin	The Confucian Temple with its main hall, Dacheng Dian, at Pingyao, Shanxi, was built.
1240	12th year, Taizong of the Mongols	The Palace of Perpetual Happiness, or Yongle Gong, was built at Yongle Town in Yongji County, Shanxi. It is a Taoist temple in memory of Lu Dongbin, one of the Eight Taoist Immortals, and it was said that Yongle Town was Lu Dongbin's birthplace.
1267	4th year, Zhiyuan,Shizu of the Mongols	The Mongol Emperor Kublai Khan moved the capital to Youzhou (present-day Beijing), and renamed it as Dadu, or the Great Capital. Liu Bingzhong was appointed to plan and construct the Great Capital.
1269	6th year, ZhiyuanShizu of the Mongols	The Imperial College (the highest educational administration) was established in Dadu (the Great Capital).
1271	8th year, Zhiyuan,Shizu of the Yuan	In Miaoying Temple, a Lamasery in Beijing, the White Dagoba, which is a pagoda in Lamaist style, was erected. It is the earliest dagoba preserved intact in China.
1275	1st year, Deyou,Gongdi, the Song	Tomb of Puhading, sixteenth generation descendent of Mohammed, was built in Yangzhou, Jiangsu. Xianhe Si (literally, the Mosque of White Crane) was erected in Yangzhou.
The Yuan Dynasty		
13th century	Early Yuan Period	The Southern Temple of Saga in Saga County, Tibet, was built.
13th century	Early Yuan Period	The Hill of Longevity and the Imperial Lake were constructed in Dadu (the Great Capital) as the Imperial Garden of the Yuan Court. The Hill of Longevity was constructed on the Jade Flower Islet (or Qionghua Island) of the Jin, which is in Beihai Park of today's Beijing.
1302	6th year, Dade, Chengzong	The Confucian Temple in Dadu (present-day Beijing) was built.
1309	2nd year, Zhida, Wuzong	The Ashab Mosque at Quanzhou, Fujian, was renovated.
1323	3rd year, Zhizhi, Yingzong	Islamic Holy Tombs of Quanzhou, Fujian, were renovated.
1342	2nd year, Zhizheng, Shundi	Tian Ru, a Buddhist abbot, built the Shizi Lin (Garden of Lion Grove) in Suzhou.
1350	10th year, Zhizheng, Shundi	Huaisheng Si, or the Mosque in Memory of the Saint, in Guangzhou was renovated.
1356	16th year, Zhizheng, Shundi	The Mosque of Dongsi in Beijing was first built. It was renovated in 1447.
1363	23rd year, Zhizheng, Shundi	Mausoleum of Tuheluk Timur at Huocheng near Gulja (Yining), Xinjiang, was built.
The Ming Dynasty		
1368	1st year, Hongwu,Taizu	The Ming Court began to construct its imperial palace in Nanjing.

Christian era	Chinese Dynastic Years	Events or Achievements
1373	6th year, Hongwu, Taizu	Construction of the Capital City of Nanjing as well as the imperial palace was completed. General Xu Da was appointed to garrison the northern frontiers. Based on Hua Yunlong's proposal, the Great Wall was first rebuilt. It was renovated and extended several times in the Ming period. Temple for Offering Sacrifices to Emperors of the Past Dynasties was built on the southern slope of Qintian Hill in Nanjing.
1376~1383	9th~15th year, Hongwu, Tai	The Main Hall of Linggu Temple, a vaulted beamless building, in Nanjing was built.
1381	14th year, Hongwu, Taizu	Construction of Xiaoling Tomb (the Mausoleum of Emperor Taizu) started in Nanjing. The tomb was completed in 1405.
1407	5th year, Yongle, Chengzu	Construction of the Forbidden City in Beijing began.
1409	7th year, Yongle, Chengzu	Construction of Changling Tomb (the Mausoleum of Emperor Yongle) began in Changping County, Beijing.
1413	11th year, Yongle, Chengzu	An imperial order was given to build Taoist building complexes in Wudang Mountain, Hubei. It took 11 years to build up 8 palaces, 2 temples, 36 nunneries and 72 cliff temples.
1420	18th year, Yongle, Chengzu	City of Beijing with the Imperial City and Forbidden City included was completed. Capital of the Ming moved to Beijing. In Beijing, the Altar of Heaven, the Altar of Earth, the Imperial Ancestral Temple and the Altar of Agriculture were built.
1421	19th year, Yongle, Chengzu	The Three Great Halls of the Forbidden City were destroyed by fire. The Altar of Land and Grain in Beijing was built.
1436	1st year, Zhengtong, Yingzong	The Three Great Halls of the Forbidden City were rebuilt.
1442	7th year, Zhengtong,Yingzong	Libai Si of Niujie, or the Mosque of Ox Street, in Beijing was renovated. The Mosque was thoroughly restored and extended in 1696.
1444	9th year, Zhengtong,Yingzong	Zhihua Temple in Beijing was built.
1447	12th year, Zhengtong,Yingzong	Tashilunpo Monastery was built in Xigaze, Tibet.
1473	9th year, Chenghua,Xianzong	Diamond Throne Pagodas (Vajrasana Pagoda, which is a five-pagoda cluster) as well as the Temple of True Awakening where the Pagodas housed were built in Beijing.
1483~1487	19th~23rd year,Chenghua, Xianzong,	The layout of Confucian Temple in Qufu, Shandong, was completed in today's range and appearance.
1506~1521	Reign Period of Zhengde, Wuzong	Jichang Garden in Wuxi, Jiangsu, was built. It was famous for its "Eight-Scaled Ravine".
1509	4th year, Zhengde, Wuzong	Wang Xianchen, a censor of the Court, dismissed from office and returned to his home town Suzhou, where he built a garden and named it "Zhuozheng Yuan" (the Humble Administrator's Garden).
1519	14th year, Zhengde, Wuzong	The Palace of Heavenly Purity and Palace of Earthly Tranquillity in the Forbidden City of Beijing, were rebuilt.
1522~1566	Reign Period of Jiajing, Shizong	Liu Yuan, or the Lingering Garden, in Suzhou was first built. It was restored in the Qing Dynasty.
1530	9th year, Jiajing, Shizong	Altar of Earth, Altar of the Sun and Altar of the Moon were constructed in the outskirts of Beijing. A series of sacrifices to Heaven, Earth, the Sun and the Moon in the four outskirts of the capital city were restored. Altar of Agriculture was rebuilt.
1531	10th year, Jiajing, Shizong	Temple for Offering Sacrifices to Emperors of the Past Dynasties was built in Beijing.
1534	13th year, Jiajing, Shizong	The Altar of Heaven and Earth in Beijing was turned into the Altar of Heaven, or the Temple of Heaven.
1537	16th year, Jiajing, Shizong	The Hall of Mental Cultivation in the Forbidden City in Beijing was newly built.
1540	19th year, Jiajing, Shizong	The Stone Pailou of the Ming Tombs in Changping, Beijing, was erected.
1545	24th year, Jiajing, Shizong	The Imperial Ancestral Temple in Beijing was rebuilt. The Main Hall of the Temple of Heaven in Beijing was rebuilt. The hall which had been rectangular in plan was changed into a triple-eaved circular building, and renamed as the Hall of Prayer for Good Harvest.
1559	38th year, Jiajing, Shizong	Being a private garden in Shanghai, Yu Yuan was built by Pan Yunduan, a retired official. The rockery there was piled up by Zhang Nanyang, a famous rockery craftsman at that time.
1568	2nd year, Longqing, Muzong	General Qi Jiguang was appointed to garrison Jizhou near Beijing. Hence the Great Wall was restored and extended, and many more beacon towers and passes were built along the Great Wall.
1573~1619	Years of Wanli, Shenzong	Mi Wanzhong built his personal garden Shao Yuan in Beijing, which was famous for its four rarities: hill, water, flowers and rocks.
1583	11th year, Wanli, Shenzong	Construction of Dingling Tomb (the Mausoleum of Emperor Wanli) in Changping, Beijing, started.

Christian era	Chinese Dynastic Years	Events or Achievements
1583	26th year, Wanli, Shenzong	The Later Jin built Xingjingling Tombs (Tombs of Imperial Ancestors of the Qing) in Xinbin, Liaoning. The Tombs were renamed as Yongling Tombs in 1659.
1615	48th year, Wanli, Shenzong	The Three Great Halls of the Forbidden City in Beijing were rebuilt.
1629	2nd year, Chongzhen, Sizong	The Later Jin built Fuling Tomb (Tomb of Nurhaci, Emperor Taizu of the Qing) in Shenyang, Liaoning.
1634	7th year, Chongzhen, Sizong	Yuan ye, a treatise on Chinese gardens written by Ji Cheng, was published.
1640	13th year, Chongzhen, Sizong	The Qing Court built Dugong Hall (the Hall of Great Power) of the Imperial Palace in Shenyang.
1643	16th year, Chongzhen, Sizong	Zhaoling Tomb (Tomb of Huangtaiji, Emperor Taizong of the Qing) was first built in Shenyang, Liaoning.
The Qing Dynasty		
1645~1911		The traditional styles of local dwelling houses what we may catch sight of today had been formed to a great extent.
17th century	Early Qing Period	Tomb of Apak Hoja (Khwaja) in Kashi, Xinjiang, was first built. The tomb underwent several renovations in later years.
1644~1661	Reign Period of Shunzhi, Shizu	The West Imperial Garden (the Three Imperial Lakes with their surroundings) was reconstructed west of the Forbidden City in Beijing. The White Dagoba was erected on the top of the hill of the Jade Flower Islet in the Northern Lake (present-day Beihai Park).
1645	2nd year, Shunzhi, Shizu	Dalai Lama the Fifth rebuilt and extended the Potala Palace in Lhasa, Tibet.
1655	12th year, Shunzhi, Shizu	The Palace of Heavenly Purity and Palace of Earthly Tranquillity of the Forbidden City in Beijing were rebuilt.
1661	18th year, Shunzhi, Shizu	The Eastern Qing Tomb in Zunhua, Hebei, began to be constructed.
1662~1722	Reign Period of Kangxi, Shengzu	Chengqi Lou, a circular dwelling of the Hakkas was built in Yongding County, Fujian.
1663	2nd year, Kangxi, Shengzu	Xiaoling Tomb (the Mausoleum of Emperor Shunzhi) was completed in the Eastern Qing Tombs in Zunhua, Hebei.
1672	11th year, Kangxi, Shengzu	Temple of Marquis Wu Xiang in memory of Zhuge Liang was built in Chengdu, Sichuan.
1677	16th year, Kangxi, Shengzu	The layout of Dai Miao (the Temple of Eastern Sacred Mountain) in Mount Tai, Shandong, was completed in today's scale.
1680	19th year, Kangxi, Shengzu	Chengxin Yuan, an imperial garden at Jade Spring Hill in the western suburbs of Beijing, was built. It was renamed as Jingming Yuan, or the Garden of Light and Tranquillity, in later years.
1681	20th year, Kangxi, Shengzu	Jingling Tomb (the Mausoleum of Emperor Kangxi) started to be constructed in the Eastern Qing Tombs in Zunhua, Hebei.
1683	22nd year, Kangxi, Shengzu	Building complex of the Hall of Literary Glory in the Forbidden City in Beijing was rebuilt.
1684	23rd year, Kangxi, Shengzu	Changchun Yuan, or the Enjoying-the-Spring Garden, was constructed in the western suburbs of Beijing.
1689	28th year, Kangxi, Shengzu	Palace of Tranquil Longevity in the Forbidden City in Beijing was built.
1690	29th year, Kangxi, Shengzu	The Hall of Supreme Harmony in the Forbidden City began to be rebuilt. The hall was completed in 1695.
1703	42nd year, Kangxi, Shengzu	Construction of the Summer Resort at Chengde, Hebei, started.
1710	49th year, Kangxi, Shengzu	Guan Di Miao, or the Temple of Lord Guan was rebuilt in Guan's birthplace Xiexian County, Shanxi.
1718	57th year, Kangxi, Shengzu	Xiaodongling Tomb (the Tomb of Empress of Shunzhi) was built to the east of Xiaoling Tomb in the Eastern Qing Tombs in Zunhua, Hebei.
1725	3rd year, Yongzheng, Shizong	Construction of Yuanming Yuan, or the Garden of Perfect Splendor, or Garden of Perfection and Brightness, started in the northwestern suburbs of Beijing. It was then extended and developed to 40 scenic spots during the period of Emperor Qianlong.
1730	8th year, Yongzheng, Shizong	Tailing Tomb (the Mausoleum of Emperor Yongzheng) was first built in Yizhou (present-day Yixian, Hebei). The Tomb was completed in 1737.
1734	12th year, Yongzheng, Shizong	The Board of Works promulgated Gongcheng Zuofa Zeli, or the Structural Regulations, as building codes for design and construction works.
1735	13th year, Yongzheng, Shizong	Fragrant Hill Summer Resort for the emperor was built in the Western Hills of Beijing.
1736~1796	Reign period of Qianlong, Gaozong	Ge Yuliang, a well-known rockery craftsman, built the Huanxiu Shanzhuang (the Nestling-in-Green Mountain Villa) in Suzhou.

Christian era	Chinese Dynastic Years	Events or Achievements
1745	10th year, Qianlong, Gaozong	Fragrant Hill Summer Resort in the western hills of Beijing was extended and renamed as Jingyi Yuan (the Garden of Congenial Tranquillity).
1746~1748	11th~13th years, Qianlong, Gaozong	The Central Palatial Complex of the Imperial Palace in Shenyang was extended. Two lodges, or building compounds, were built and added to the east and west of the Central Complex.
1750	15th year, Qianlong, Gaozong	The Pavilion of the Rain of Flowers was erected in the Forbidden City in Beijing. Construction of Qingyi Yuan, or the Garden of Clear Ripples, started. It was an imperial garden including the Hill of Longevity and the Kunming Lake in the western suburbs of Beijing. It took 14 years to complete this garden.
1751	16th year, Qianlong, Gaozong	Changchun Yuan (the Garden of Eternal Spring) and Qichun Yuan (the Garden of Blossoming Spring) were built to the east of Yuanming Yuan (the Garden of Perfect Splendor).
1752	17th year, Qianlong, Gaozong	Roofing tiles of the Hall of Prayer for Good Harvest in the Temple of Heaven, Beijing, were rebuilt with blue glazed tiles. The Imperial Palace in Shenyang was renovated.
1755	20th year, Qianlong, Gaozong	Puning Si (Temple of Universal Tranquillity), in Chengde, Hebei, was built. Its main hall, Dacheng Ge (Pavilion of Mahayana) was built to imitate the main hall of Sangye Temple in Tibet.
1764	29th year, Qianlong, Gaozong	Anyuan Miao Temple in Chengde, Hebei, was Built.
1765	30th year, Qianlong, Gaozong	Song Zongyuan, a retired official, built Wangshi Yuan, or the Garden of the Master of Fishing Nets, in Suzhou.
1766	31st year, Qianlong,	Pule Si Temple in Chengde, Hebei, was built.
1767~1771	32nd~36th years, Qianlong, Gaozong	Temple of the Potaraka Doctrine (Putuo Zongcheng Zhi Miao) in Chengde, Hebei, was built.
1774	39th year, Qianlong, Gaozong	Wenyuan Ge Library in the Forbidden City, Beijing, was built.
1778	43rd year, Qianlong, Gaozong	The Western Palatial Complex of the Imperial Palace in Shenyang was built. The Mosque with Su Gong Tower in Turpan, Xinjiang, was completed.
1779~1780	44th~45th years, Qianlong, Gaozong	Temple of Sumeru Happiness and Longevity (Xu Mi Fu Shou Zhi Miao) in Chengde, Hebei, was built.
1781	46th year, Qianlong, Gaozong	Wensu Ge Library, Yangxi Zhai Study and Jiayin Tang Hall of the Imperial Palace in Shenyang were built.
1783	48th year, Qianlong, Gaozong	Biyong, or the Main Hall of the Imperial College (Guo Zi Jian), in Beijing was built.
1784	49th year, Qianlong, Gaozong	Dagobas of the City of Complete Purification (Qing Jing Hua Cheng Ta) of the West Yellow Temple in Beijing were erected.
18th century		Taer Temple in Huangzhong, Qinghai, was built.
1796	1st year, Jiaqing, Renzong	Changling Tomb (the Mausoleum of Emperor Jiaqing) of t h e Western Qing Tombs in Yixian, Hebei, was first built. It was completed eight years later.
1804	9th year, Jiaqing, Renzong	Three Palatial Complexes with Lodges of the Central Complex of the Imperial Palace in Shenyang were renovated.
1832	12th year, Daoguang, Renzong	Muling Tomb (the Mausoleum of Emperor Daoguang) of the Western Qing Tombs in Yixian, Hebei, was first built. It was completed four years later.
1859	9th year, Xianfeng, Wenzong	Dingling Tomb (the Mausoleum of Emperor Xianfeng) of the Eastern Qing Tombs in Zunhua, Hebei, was first built.
1860	10th year, Xianfeng, Wenzong	Yuanming Yuan (the Garden of Perfect Splendor) and Qingyi Yuan (the Garden of Clear Ripples) were destroyed and burnt down by the Anglo-French Allied forces.
1873	12th year, Tongzhi, Muzong	Dingdongling Tombs (Tombs of Empress Dowagers Cixi and Ci'an) were first built in the Eastern Qing Tombs in Zunhua, Hebei. The Tombs were completed in 1879.
1875	1st year, Guangxu, Dezong	Huiling Tomb (the Mausoleum of Emperor Tongzhi) of the Eastern Qing Tombs in Zunhua, Hebei, was built.
1888	14th year, Guangxu, Dezong	Qingyi Yuan was rebuilt and renamed as Yihe Yuan (the Summer Palace) under Empress Dowager Cixi. Jianfu Palace of Qingcheng Mountain, Sichuan, was rebuilt.
1909	1st year, Xuantong	Chongling Tomb (the Mausoleum of Emperor Guangxu) was built in the Western Qing Tombs in Yixian, Hebei.

The Excellence of Ancient Chinese Architecture, Chinese Edition
Author: Wang Qijun
Chief Planner: Zhou Yi
Editorial Members: Wang Boyang, Wei Ran, Wang Xuelin
Editor in Charge: Wang Boyang, Zhang Zhenguang, Fei Hailing
Photographers: Zhang Zhenguang, Wei Ran, Chen Xiaoli, Li Dongxi, Cao Yang

The Excellence of Ancient Chinese Architecture, English Edition
Chief Planner: Zhang Huizhen
Translators: Mo Runxian, Zhang Mintai, San Mu
Editor in Charge: Qi Linlin, Zhang Huizhen
Photographers: Zhang Zhenguang, Wei Ran, Chen Xiaoli, Li Dongxi, Cao Yang
Cover Design: Fu Jinhong
Layout Design: Xiao Jinxing

The Excellence of
Ancient Chinese Architecture

Vernacular Dwellings 民間居內建築
Earth Dwellings, Cave Dwellings and Siheyuan Compound

Wang Qijun

© 2012 China Architecture & Building Press
Published and Distributed by China Architecture & Building Press
ISBN 978-7-112-14114-2 (22171)
CIP data available on request
www.cabp.com.cn

Printed on acid-free and chlorine-free bleached paper

Printed in China